A People So Bold

A People So Bold

Theology and Ministry for Unitarian Universalists

John Gibb Millspaugh, Editor

SKINNER HOUSE BOOKS
BOSTON

 Published by Skinner House Books, an imprint of the Unitarian Universalist Association of Congregations, a liberal religious organization with more than 1,000 congregations in the U.S. and Canada, 25 Beacon St., Boston, MA 02108-2800.

Printed in the United States

Cover and text design by Suzanne Morgan

ISBN 1-55896-552-1
978-1-55896-552-2

12 11 10 09
6 5 4 3 2 1

Library of Congress Cataloging-in-Publication Data
A people so bold : theology and ministry for Unitarian Universalists / John Gibb Millspaugh, editor.
p. cm.
ISBN-13: 978-1-55896-552-2 (alk. paper)
ISBN-10: 1-55896-552-1 (alk. paper)
1. Unitarian Universalist Association—Doctrines. 2. Social justice—Religious aspects—Unitarian Universalist Association. I. Millspaugh, John Gibb.
BX9841.3.P46 2009
261.8—dc22
2009022691

Contents

Introduction

Until recently, when asked which conversation in Unitarian Universalist history I would most like to overhear—if I could fling myself back through the centuries and linger unnoticed among any group—I have answered, "the Symposium."

When I cheat by choosing a series of more than thirty conversations, no one seems to mind. How could I answer otherwise? That nineteenth-century group of New England activists, scholars, educators, and rebel Unitarian ministers, who lightheartedly called themselves "the Club of the Like-Minded" because no two could ever fully agree, gathered with no slighter goal than fomenting social and religious reform—and they succeeded.

Although the Symposium only met from 1836 to 1840; although the group's detractors smeared its conversations as too abstract and "transcendentalist"; although its import was widely dismissed until decades after it dissolved, the conversations among Ralph Waldo Emerson, Margaret Fuller, Henry David Thoreau, Elizabeth Peabody, Bronson Alcott, and more than forty others led to a revolution within Unitarianism. Many of the Symposium's members also went on to pioneer national social reform. As historian Megan Marshall writes in *The Peabody Sisters*, the Symposium's conversations changed these disaffected religionists, preoccupied with abstractions, into "a mixed band of reformers, male and female, ready to preach a cause." The causes they preached were as radical as free universal education, women's rights, prison reform, antimonopoly legislation, poverty reduction, and elimination of debtor prisons. Although what came to be known as the Transcendental Club still today connotes vague metaphysical discussions, its careful conversations produced thought and action that forever changed American religion and society.

In all of Unitarian and Universalist history, where and when would *you* choose to eavesdrop? Perhaps another era, another place. Before you answer, let me introduce you to the convocation that changed my longstanding response to the question. It took place in Baltimore, Maryland, in early 2009, just before Barack Obama's inauguration as president. The gathering happened so recently that we cannot yet know its implications for either our religion or our country.

The thirty-six participants in the Baltimore convocation came from California, Colorado, Illinois, Massachusetts, Minnesota, Oregon, Texas, and Virginia. They represented the silent generation, the baby boom, and generations X and Y. Their number included the Unitarian Universalist Association president and the two candidates competing to succeed him; congregation ministers, ministers of social justice, music directors, and youth directors; directors of the UU Service Committee and the Center for the Study of Religious Freedom; UUA staff specializing in advocacy and witness; scholars and representatives from five seminaries and divinity schools; men and women, Asian and black and Latino and white Americans, bisexual, gay, lesbian, and straight people—religious leaders all.

They gathered to talk about how Unitarian Universalism could move beyond its emphasis on "freedom from"—freedom from creeds, dogmas, idolatries of the mind and spirit—to "freedom for"—what our faith calls us to do, how we put our faith into action. They considered how UU faith grounds our work for social justice. How it holds brokenness, injustice, and suffering, and how and whether it names or confronts evil. How UU people and institutions develop effective, prophetic engagement with the issues of our day.

Participants wrestled with these topics in essays they traded before the gathering. This volume collects the final, post-conference versions of their essays, and the companion DVD (also titled *A People So Bold*), captures the highlights of the conversations. I have arranged the book so that each paper flows naturally from the one before it, in some cases picking up a thread from the last one, in others, starting to sew in a new direction.

The first part of this book, Theology, identifies UU faith commitments that inspire and guide our work for positive change. Meg Riley's essay reclaims the term *prophetic* for liberal religion, setting the stage for the word's use throughout the book. Paul Rasor provides six theological foundations for UU justice work, and he names three tensions in Unitarian Universalism that cause us, at times, to "stumble over our own best intentions." Dan McKanan sees hope in our historic practices of interfaith conversation and discipleship, and potential roadblocks in our association's fixation with congregations, our congregations' preoccupation with growth, and our individual reluctance to learn from people we would more comfortably ignore.

As if in response, Nancy McDonald Ladd asks what UUs can learn from Lutheran pastor Walter Rauschenbusch, the Christian Realist movement, and the Unitarian theologian who responded to both: James Luther Adams, who said Unitarians will never become effective change agents until we take seriously the reality of evil. In "Resisting Evil, Reverencing Life," Rebecca Parker advises UUs to confront evil face-to-face—in ourselves, in others, and in institutions—that we might destroy it, contain it, and transform it. While Sharon Welch agrees with portions of Parker's analysis, she rejects its Western, dualistic sense of good and evil, to join with those for whom "the attempt to destroy evil is seen as a form of insanity." Drawing on wisdom from sources beyond the dominant culture, Welch points to the work beckoning us today: building and governing just institutions.

The second part, Context, opens with Kat Liu's stark contrasts between today's postmodern, multiethnic society and our religious movement's "generally tepid appeal to people of color," asking, "What, then, will we be, and for whom? If we want to be a religion of the race and class privileged, then we need not change, and we can watch society pass us by." Robert Hardies sees another way, and he uses the tortured and glorious history of a particular street corner to reflect on how dance might call us to revolution. Adam Gerhardstein confounds Meg Riley's earlier definition of the prophetic (as linking past, present, and future) by agreeing with Parker that prophetic faith must not focus "on how far we have come or how far we have to go but on where we are now."

Thandeka narrows the focus further, from our present circumstances to human feeling, arguably both the context and the goal of our justice work. In a case study of Washington Mutual bank's culpability in the recent recession, she argues that since economic injustice involves the abuse of souls, effective work for economic justice protects souls and restores them to health. Marilyn Sewell sees the source of our economic problems as a distortion of the dream upon which our nation's government was founded. That dream always has been limited and flawed, but now it has twisted into something spiritually vapid and morally bankrupt, "not a dream worthy of our lives." Sewell puts faith in our creative capacity to foster new cultures of service, integrity, and covenant. Peter Morales agrees that we cannot understand our role in today's America of "the moo-shoo burrito and the Korean taco" unless we understand the effects of history, policy, and religion—for example, the historic tracing of the Mexican-American border to accommodate slavery, the current U.S. policies contributing to "wrenching economic dislocations in Mexico, Guatemala, and Nicaragua," and most importantly, the religious wisdom calling humanity to live as one people.

The third part, Ministry, turns to the practical, describing how UU justice theologies deployed in today's context can create effective ministries of worship, music, small groups, education, and youth programs, all contributing to positive social change. Rather than explicating specific justice issues (which are ever-shifting), this section focuses on creating and sustaining communities that can effectively address themselves to those issues. Victoria Safford argues for congregations to understand themselves as keepers of "sacred stories," especially when those stories are hard to hear, revealing beauty or ugliness, truth or falsehood. William Sinkford agrees, noting that Unitarian Universalism has too long told its story in black and white terms—not only racially, but also as if UUs can do only right or only wrong. Neither approach suffices, and if we are to remain relevant we need to claim our power to choose more robust models. To find these models, Jill Schwendeman looks to UU youth who are already "living their own new stories," reflecting on how their vibrant faith enlivens her own faith and how work with adolescents reveals the still-growing edges of Unitarian Universalism.

Mark Hicks shifts the focus from narratives to lived experiences. He knows from years teaching adult learners that deep change usually results not from shifting what we think, but how we think. Alida DeCoster agrees that we learn best when we balance mind with heart and action with reflection, and she finds models in the weekly theological reflection groups for interns at the UUA's Washington Office for Advocacy. Paula Cole Jones's essay follows, focusing on the factors that equip congregations to effectively engage "the struggle to reconcile injustice and embrace the multicultural community." Taquiena Boston's heart breaks as she wanders the chasm dividing UU congregations from black churches, and she tells stories from each community to illustrate their unconnected efforts to wed compassion to justice.

Carol Caouette also focuses on congregations' work for justice, but with an ear to the sanctuary music that can "electrify space, transform us emotionally, and propel us beyond our ordinary lives" to encounter the holy, which inspires work beyond the sanctuary walls. Kate Lore meditates on love's central role in justice work. She names *covenant* as the chalice in which we offer love to one another and to the world, and provides practical advice for social action committees. In the final essay, Rob Keithan argues that our congregations' devotion to meaning and community is rounded out by a commitment to justice—we improve any congregational program when we ask how it can better serve all three. Louise Green's benediction focuses on the essential question, What matters? Her spare phrases call us to praxis, action interwoven with reflection. All of which brings us back to where we started.

Like members of the Transcendental Club, participants in the Baltimore convocation began more conversations than they could complete. They sometimes disagreed, and many who might have provided key insights never made it to the table. Undoubtedly, some issues that future generations will recognize as vital went virtually unaddressed. Revelations were partial. Yet we in the twenty-first century can learn something from the case of the Transcendental Club. It was not primarily the talk within that group but what happened in response to it that changed the history of religion and society. The conversation expanded from the Symposium's first gathering of male ministers and divinity students to include educators, then women, and then other activists. Even as the group disbanded in 1840, members such as Margaret Fuller and Bronson Alcott were inspired to launch their own conversation circles. The publications of club members' essays in *The Dial* and elsewhere prompted reflection, commendation, disgust, enthusiasm, and outrage throughout the movement. It was less the Symposium itself than Unitarians' engagement with the ideas it generated that pushed the work forward.

Therefore, it is not the Baltimore convocation but your response that will determine the effect of these conversations on future generations. Perhaps you will let the ideas in this volume sit on a shelf. Perhaps you will select one key paragraph as a focus for a small-group session in your congregation, or pick a paragraph from each essay, create a year or two's worth of small-group ministry programs, and post them online to be used throughout the Association. Perhaps you will hand a few essays to new members of your social action committee as part of their orientation, or ask your congregational board to read the book and articulate its vision for social action. Perhaps you will deliver a sermon on what you find here that most inspires you. Perhaps you will start a blog to point out flaws in the book or create content to fill the gaps. In other words, perhaps you will make these transforming ideas matter.

Many versions of the word *transform* appear throughout this volume. I invite you to interpret the term not in its grandiose sense—creating a new future almost completely disconnected from the past—but as the kind of momentous change that occurs in nature as the result of slight adaptations. In biological evolution, as leadership theorist Ronald Heifetz points out in a 1999 interview, an adaptation leaving well over 99 percent of the genetic code intact can transform "in the sense that it dramatically widens, deepens, and broadens capacity to thrive in new environments . . . [changing] even what thriving *means* in terms of the values that we stand for and the values that we hold in our aspirations." In the case of species, individuals, or institutions, most DNA is worth keeping. Transformation happens when we carry forward the wisdom of the past and make relatively tiny adaptations to meet the challenges of the new environment. So even if UUs form less than 1 percent of our country's current population (as we do), and even if only a small percentage of UUs read this book, and a small percentage of readers act on what they find in these pages, that is enough to engender an adaptation that can transform our faith and nation.

Today, if I could choose to eavesdrop on any conversation in UU history, it would be those chronicled in *A People So Bold*. This is because I live in this age and have the capacity to affect it. You and I have not arrived at the end of history but stand in its very midst; we can affect generations to come. Historians call 1836, the founding year of the Symposium, the Unitarian *Annus Mirabilis*, the Year of Wonders. Perhaps our efforts for social change will justify future chronicles calling 2011 the Year of Works—the *Año de Obras*. And if you notice that phrase isn't Latin, you're already getting the point these essays make about relevance.

May we recognize ourselves as a people worthy of all who have come before us, a people with the power to respond to the challenges of our era, a people who join hands within and beyond our congregations to work for a better future; may we be, in short, a people so bold.

John Gibb Millspaugh
December 2009

Prophetic Congregations in the Twenty-First Century

MEG RILEY

What relevance could the ancient word *prophetic* still hold for Unitarian Universalists? The term mostly bewilders us, conjuring images of wild-eyed, ranting men with long white beards holding signs proclaiming "The end is near," foretelling apocalyptic vengeance courtesy of God the Father.

Certainly Unitarian Universalism has grown past *that* image. Many Unitarian Universalists would abandon the idea of the prophetic entirely. I have heard UUs speak instead of congregations that are bold, or visionary, or relevant, or vital, or justice-seeking. I like all those words, but I like *prophetic* more, because of its relationship to time and possibility; it draws from a place deep in our past and casts our vision around the corner into an unknown future. The word is useful when it transcends doom-and-gloom "The end is near" proclamations and instead declares, "The beginning is near!" It is useful when it calls us to create something new, even now. This is the prophetic in the sense used by twentieth-century Unitarian theologian James Luther Adams, who called on us to take responsibility to see the consequences of our behavior "with the intention of making history rather than being pushed around by it."

In this sense of prophetic, then, we might reflect on how our quirky jewel of a faith could respond to this historic moment. I have cast my lot with Unitarian Universalism not just because it is where I am called to be; I am here because, while decades of interfaith work have shown me that ours are not the only prophetic congregations, UU faith communities are some of the most creative and potentially powerful institutions in our nation. The need is great, so our understanding the prophetic church today is an urgent matter.

Prophetic UU congregations share three central characteristics. First, they draw from the deepest parts of Unitarian and Universalist theology, committing themselves to the wisdom of those theologies. Our work to cocreate the holy in this world is most effective when it builds on the perspectives gained by the hard experience of those who came before us. Prophetic congregations draw strength for today through connecting to the essential insights and actions of our ancestors. Second, prophetic congregations embody radical caring—radical in the sense of the very roots of the place, its central mission. You sometimes hear *caring*, the pastoral aspect of congregations, described as the opposite of prophetic, but this dualism is false and destructive. Radical caring is both prophetic and pastoral. Third, while drawing on our past and on caring in the present, prophetic congregations orient themselves squarely toward the future. Prophetic eyes see through the lens of hope—not hope born from naïveté, or from casting our gazes away from oppression and suffering, but hope as a spiritually disciplined response to the whole, a commitment to action. Each of these three aspects deserves more explanation.

Prophetic congregations are thoroughly committed to understanding and grappling with Unitarian, Universalist, and Unitarian Universalist understandings of ultimate reality. Our theology is deeply incarnational: our faith and spirituality are based in earthly, this-world, daily engagement with the holy. Each night a child is born is holy, we say, rather than locating holiness only in the birth of Jesus. There is a priesthood of all believers, we say, rather than locating all wisdom in those who are ordained. UUs understand salvation to take place not elsewhere, after we are dead, but in our daily choices today, in this world. The world is not an evil, sinful place we would be lucky to leave for some pure, godly place. Come what may after our deaths, we have cast our lot with those gods and mortals committed to creating together what is holy right here in the incomprehensibly beautiful, horrifically broken, frighteningly vulnerable, miraculous place we call home.

Consider our legacy from the early Universalists. In 1803, the very first time they gathered, they affirmed that no loving God—no God worthy of their worship—would have created people in order to enslave them. They knew the living experience of a loving God, and so they rejected slavery not as a political position but as a religious affirmation. They simply stood on the side of love. Two centuries later, we struggle with the implications of that radical understanding.

To commit to creating a prophetic congregation today is to grapple with what it means to take responsibility for cocreating the holy right here on earth. This is no small demand; it is much harder than agreeing with a particular belief. I am bewildered by those who think Unitarian Universalism is an easy faith! For us, faith is not something we own—our only real possessions, as the Buddhist monk Thich Nhat Han says, are our actions. We believe in deeds, not creeds. We believe that God's primary domain is here, not elsewhere, and that faith is to be known and salvation found in our daily actions, not in our proclamations about what it might be like elsewhere. That is point one.

Prophetic congregations must also be places of radical caring. A recent Duke University study documents that between 1985 and 2004, the number of people with whom the average American discussed "important matters" dropped from three to two. Even more stunning, almost 25 percent of those surveyed said there was *no one* with whom they discussed important matters. The number of those folks has tripled since 1985. Also, the 2000 census revealed that 25 percent of Americans now live alone, up from 7 percent in 1940.

Given today's cultural context, visionary churches will be places where people come into genuine, full-spirited, embodied contact with one another. We provide a healing balm when we create covenant groups, support groups, parent groups, faith development opportunities, youth groups, and other places where people can relax into real relationship with one another. Real relationships mean those that go beyond superficial or serial socializing to build authentic community.

Recently, the young people in my office insisted I join Facebook, a social network on the Internet. As of this writing, I have 628 Facebook "friends." I write "friends" with skepticism because as much as I enjoy electronic interaction, I have never even met many of these people. Facebook is engaging enough to easily take up all my time, so that I might never sink into the much more frustrating, confounding, and rewarding conversations available only through real friendships or a covenanted partnership. By midlife, I have figured out that every person I love is truly, deeply flawed and difficult. These people are annoying and frustrating—but they are also brilliant, beautiful, and uniquely gifted. When I was younger, I kept expecting this to change, that someday I would trade in these friends for easier ones—people who were kind and sane and purely good. Now I look in the mirror and say, "Honey, if those people existed, they would take a pass on you!" Virtual communities cannot substitute for communion with the real.

A few years ago, as I was leaving for yet another business trip, I said to my three-year-old daughter, "I'll still be here in your heart while I'm gone." She replied, "But my heart can't smell you, or hold your hand." At age fifty-three, the preciousness of embodiment is clearer to me than it once was. While I adore Facebook (I admit it), please come lock me up if I ever confuse it with friends I can call in the middle of the night when I am consumed with terror, grief, or shame. Throw my computer out the window if I ever tell you that typing "LOL" (Internet shorthand for "laughing out loud") is a good substitute for sitting on the couch with a friend, howling with laughter till we cry.

Radical caring calls us to create truly inclusive congregations. Many Unitarian Universalists can name the time when, because of a deepening connection to our faith community, we were suddenly able to relax, to know that all our edges were accepted, that we did not have to choose which of our identities we could safely allow into the room. How do our congregations let people know that they are in such places—especially in today's landscape, with its variety of cultures, languages, musical forms, metaphors, stories, political analyses, and other differences?

In the planes and buses and taxis that schlep me around for my job, I engage in passing conversations with a lot of people. I don't shy away from talking about Unitarian Universalism, because I know from experience that this faith saves lives. Many of those most interested in Unitarian Universalism cross the borders of various communities. Perhaps they are Muslims married to Hindus, or Christians married to Jews. Perhaps they love someone of their own sex, but are part of a heterosexist community or culture. Perhaps they identify as transgender or multiracial. People who cross borders perk up when they hear about our faith—this multi-metaphored place of meaning-making where we approach new frontiers and welcome new revelations each day.

In my heart, I celebrate each one of these conversations, but always some amount of fear rises up as well. If my acquaintances go to a UU congregation, will they be seen as the gift that they are and invited into the community of caring, or will they be ignored? Will they have yet one more experience in life that tells them there is no basket wide enough to hold them?

To be prophetic in the twenty-first century, congregations must commit to going beyond tepid, silent, "open door" inclusion. They must commit to living engagement with one another, to learning about the complexities of each other's lives, to enjoying the vitality that difference can offer. Prophetic congregations go beyond just keeping the door open—they offer genuine mutuality to all who walk through it.

The third aspect of a prophetic congregation is a community of hope. I don't mean optimism. There is an old joke about optimism: Two identical twins are presented on their birthday with a large room full of horse manure. The pessimist cries out, "Horse manure! I should have expected this," and he sinks to the floor and begins to weep. The optimist, though, sticks both hands in the pile and begins digging. "What do you think you are doing?" bawls the pessimist. "With all this manure," replies the optimist, "there's bound to be a pony in here somewhere!"

That's optimism, not hope. A hopeful person would not pretend she had been given anything other than a room full of horse manure. But after adjusting to that dubious discovery, hope would call her to reflect on what she could do with it. She might set about converting it to biofuel, or growing a garden with it, or selling it and saving the money for a pony, or otherwise converting it to serve life's potential.

Our congregations must be places where hope is understood as an existential choice, cultivated as a spiritual discipline, and offered through concrete forms of action. Prophetic congregations put forward multiple opportunities for existential hope to emerge from joint action—people bearing together what we cannot bear alone. Often, this begins with simply witnessing what seems awful—witnessing it with others instead of alone at the computer. It begins with watching what gives life and what drains life, and naming it in community. Then, as the Hebrew scripture tell us in Deuteronomy 30:19, it requires choosing: "I have set before you life and death, blessings and curses. Choose life." The third element of prophetic church is choosing to act, in service of a better future.

Prophetic UU congregations are grounded in centuries-old theologies, which teach that we have the power and responsibility to cocreate what is holy. They are communities where we and others are deeply valued and mutually known. Prophetic congregations refuse to accept brokenness as a final answer, but work from realistic hope, choosing life, choosing to be a blessing.

The work that is necessary to create a prophetic congregation is never easy. We continually fall short, failing our purpose and one another multiple times. Yet unless we try to live up to our ideals, complete failure is guaranteed. At the end of my life, I want to look back and know that I gave all that I had, that my actions—my only true possessions—have been gladly given and gladly received. I want to be part of a faith that dares to dream big and to put those dreams, however incompletely realized, into action. So in case you haven't noticed, I'm holding a sign: "The beginning is near!" As much as it ever has been or ever will be for any person of any epoch, now is the time for us to build the prophetic church.

Identity, Covenant and Commitment

PAUL RASOR

We cannot create a prophetic church unless we know who we are. We must intentionally reclaim our religious identity. We need to know why, and be able to say why, this is *religious* work—yet a significant number of Unitarian Universalists resist identifying as religious beings, especially in public. This resistance cuts us off from our heritage and weakens our prophetic practice. To succeed in the long run, we will need constructive Unitarian Universalist theologies.

Reclaiming our religious identity requires recovering and naming the core theological principles that ground us as a movement. As Meg Riley put it during the Baltimore convocation, "we need to articulate a visionary theology of who we are—and who we are in the world."

A widespread yearning for theological deepening infuses Unitarian Universalism today—a sense that we have spent far too many years wandering in the wilderness. We sense that we must move beyond simply helping individuals build their own theologies, important though that is. We need to nurture our communal spirit by working together, with our differences, to uncover the deeper shared religious values and theological principles that lie beneath our individual theological orientations. We need to find, clarify, and perhaps rename these deeper principles for our time.

To realize the full potential of our prophetic voice, we can and must meet this challenge while respecting our differences and avoiding any hint of a creed. Despite our enormous and healthy theological diversity, we can all call ourselves Unitarian Universalists for a reason. I offer the following theological principles (drawn from my essay on Unitarianism in *The Cambridge Dictionary of Christian Theology*) as conversation starters.

The fundamental unity and interdependence of all existence. Reality is continuously re-created in a dynamic, open-ended evolutionary process.

The transforming power of love. Unitarian Universalists have always affirmed the reality of love as a dynamic and transformative relational power that exists within us and among us. This power moves us to create relationships of compassion, respect, mutuality, and forgiveness.

Human freedom, grounded in the inherent worth and dignity of all persons. Within the constraints of biological, historical, and cultural circumstance, human beings are free moral agents who are accountable for their choices. Our freedom is expressed in our striving for meaningful and fulfilling lives and for liberation from all forms of oppression. Human freedom is morally neutral; it can be used for good or for evil. Human beings have the moral capacity to make different choices and to create different institutions.

Principled theological openness. Religious truth is not given just once for all time; no belief system or historical moment has any unique status. Religious meaning is constructed rather than given and may come through many sources.

Commitment to social justice. Just communities reflect equal concern for all, respect for basic human rights and liberties, noncoercive institutions, consensual relationships, shared power, and inclusiveness. Human beings have a religious obligation to create institutions and social structures that reflect these values and enable all persons to live with dignity and respect.

The church as a free covenanted fellowship. The free church emphasizes local autonomy in church governance, nonhierarchical forms of ecclesial organization, and shared authority in decision making; it does not require uniformity of belief.

Other principles could be named. We need to have conversations and arguments about them and continue this process over time.

A theological category deserving our close attention is ecclesiology. We cannot create a prophetic church without a deeper shared understanding of what *church* is. Unitarian Universalist ecclesiology begins with the concept of covenant: a contract based on mutual obligation. In religious contexts, these commitments are understood as sacred, and covenant becomes a vehicle for defining group identity. Covenant starts with the premises that we are a free church and that we have come together voluntarily around a set of shared values in order to form a religious community.

Yet our understanding of covenant should not stop with congregational organization or polity. Polity matters—we would be far different if not for our commitment of mutual support as autonomous congregations and individuals—but covenant requires content as well as structure. If we stop with polity, we have not fully described the kind of community we have freely formed.

Covenant helps clarify our religious identity if we take it seriously enough to specify its terms. What is the content of our Unitarian Universalist covenant? What, exactly, are we are promising, and to whom? What are we committing ourselves to do? When new members join our congregations, what are they signing on to? What expectations do we have of them, and what might they reasonably expect of us? Is it simply a vague feeling of comfort and camaraderie, a general expectation to provide a supportive community for our individual spiritual journeys, or is there more to it than that?

Our covenant includes a fundamental commitment to social justice, as is clear in both the language of our Principles and Purposes and the historical practices of our tradition. Our approach to prophetic practice might look different if we truly understood it as a covenant obligation—as one of the clauses in our sacred contract with each other—rather than simply as volunteer work that we might or might not decide to take on. Although not every member would take to the streets (we all have our own gifts, and not everyone is suited for this kind of work), all members would express and celebrate prophetic social justice work as a central part of the congregation's religious identity when they sign on to the covenant. As James Luther A[illegible]ls us in *The Prophethood of All Be*[illegible]ple responsible not only for huma[illegible]cter of our institutions, and espec[illegible]or at the gate." From an ecclesiolo[illegible]nsibility is more than a general ob[illegible]of the deeper covenant commitme[illegible]us identity.

A cove[illegible]tic justice work creates commi[illegible] reach beyond the covenanting community. When we commit to creating just communities and social structures, we treat our communities and the larger society as parties to our covenant—or at least what lawyers would call third-party beneficiaries. This is an odd sort of commitment structure, since the larger society has made no reciprocal promises to us other than what is promised by the First Amendment. However, this commitment is an important part of our self-understanding as a religious community. By making prophetic practice an explicit term of our mutual covenant obligations, we define our collective religious identity as relevant beyond the doors of our meeting houses and promise one another we will work to make the world beyond our own community more just.

Finally, our covenant provides a basis for holding ourselves accountable to each other for the commitments we have made. Our prophetic voice is often directed outward, but it may also be directed inward, calling ourselves to account for the justice work we do and fail to do. Moreover, because our covenant includes obligations to the larger society, we can consider ourselves accountable to society itself—particularly to the communities on which our justice work focuses, listening to their voices as we evaluate and adjust our practices. At a deeper level, we are accountable to the shared theological convictions by which we have named ourselves, and which constitute the heart of our covenant. In all these ways, our prophetic church becomes a community of accountability.

Unitarian Universalism, like other forms of religious liberalism, contains several theological tensions that can interfere with our prophetic practice by causing us to stumble over our own best intentions. Paradoxically, many tensions are byproducts of our greatest strengths. If we wish to sustain effective prophetic practice, we need to recognize and understand these tensions.

Unitarian Universalism is characterized by theological openness that emphasizes free religious inquiry and autonomous judgment in matters of faith. This commitment is grounded in the liberal understanding that religious authority is located in individual reason and experience rather than in any external source such as the church or the Bible. For Unitarian Universalists, no claim of truth can be accepted simply because it is steeped in tradition or because the church or some other established authority declares it.

As a result, Unitarian Universalists tend to have an open-ended approach to our faith commitments. We are quite comfortable, for example, with the notions that religious doctrines change over time, that religious meaning is constructed rather than given, and that truth (or revelation) is continuously unfolding. By the same token, our faith is not likely to be threatened by new scientific discoveries or advances in biblical scholarship. Rather than resisting such developments, Unitarian Universalists and other religious liberals tend to embrace them and incorporate them into their worldviews. This principled theological openness is one of liberalism's great strengths. With its roots in our commitment to intellectual honesty, theological openness helps our faith stay credible and relevant to the needs of our time.

This open-endedness also contributes to a tendency to hold religious commitments lightly, which can make us unsure of our religious identity. We might call this the liberal fear of being pinned down. In *On Being Human Religiously*, Adams quipped that openness, without more articulation, "can produce the mind that is simply open at both ends." His point is that religious liberals are often reluctant to embrace the firm religious commitments that sustain a strong prophetic practice.

A related tension arises from our enormous theological diversity. At its best, this diversity is mutually enriching and contributes to an atmosphere of invitation in our congregations. Yet we tend to see our diversity as an expression of freedom of conscience and individual autonomy. Thus, although we encourage each other in our personal searches for truth and meaning, we often avoid communal affirmations. We easily fall prey to the postmodern cultural tendency to commodify religious faith. This move weakens our ability to create a prophetic church and, ironically, devalues the very claims of faith that we seek to welcome.

Furthermore, the search for truth can, in practice, threaten the very theological openness that invites it. Members may be subtly discouraged from searching too deeply because we mistakenly equate depth with narrowness. Unitarian Universalists may also hesitate to proclaim beliefs with too much conviction for fear of excluding or disrespecting other views. Deep engagement with theological difference can feel dangerous, and we often fall back on the safety of polite tolerance, unwittingly adopting a kind of theological "don't ask, don't tell" policy. Our reluctance to make strong religious commitments weakens our prophetic voice. Fearing to say something that might offend someone, we often say nothing.

Our collective suspicion of public religious discourse is also a source of tension. Unitarian Universalists are not bashful; as a group we tend to be highly verbal, and we have never been shy about speaking out on public issues. Yet we often seem unwilling to provide religious reasons for our public witness, and this weakens our prophetic practice. I recently surveyed more than thirty denominational resolutions and actions of immediate witness relating to issues of war and peace dating back to 1961, and found that most read like political policy platforms rather than statements of religious conviction. None offer any theological grounding; only six even bother to mention any of the Principles.

One reason for this reticence is a lack of theological clarity. Another is that many Unitarian Universalists are reluctant to speak religiously in public contexts—especially outside denominational gatherings—because we do not want to appear "too religious." Over the past quarter century, the most visible and vocal religious groups in America have been aligned with the religious right. Unitarian Universalists and other religious liberals resist religious language to avoid the conservative associations with being publicly religious today. By the same token, liberal commitment to tolerance and free religious inquiry encourages us to avoid even the appearance of proselytizing, which we tend to associate with conservative evangelicalism. While understandable, this is unfortunate. It cedes the public religious space to the loudest and most conservative speakers and effectively silences the liberal prophetic voice.

Recently some encouraging signs suggest that a revitalized religious left is emerging. According to Laura R. Olson in her essay "Whither the Religious Left?" the term *religious left* normally refers to religious people who hold liberal or progressive political views regardless of theological orientation. Many of the more vocal proponents of the religious left today hold distinctly nonliberal theologies. Still, most Unitarian Universalists would be considered part of the religious left, and we should be among its leading public voices. Yet we are not. Overcoming our suspicion of public religious discourse will not only strengthen our own practice, it may put us in conversation with those speaking prophetically from other faith perspectives, creating possibilities for collaborative justice work.

We cannot strengthen our prophetic practice unless we reclaim its religious dimensions. Our prophetic practice is rooted in the theological principles and mutual obligations that shape our covenant and define our shared faith tradition. We need to speak out not simply as liberals, but as religious liberals. Supporting liberal causes and taking liberal positions on political and social issues are not enough—we need to show that these positions are religiously grounded. We need to come out of our religious closets. Reclaiming our religious voice will strengthen our justice-making activities and help reestablish Unitarian Universalism's critical prophetic role in an era that badly needs it.

The Sacred Fire

DAN McKANAN

Unitarian Universalists can take pride in our two traditions' heritage of struggle for social justice. In her 1790 essay "On the Equality of the Sexes," Judith Sargent Murray challenged the "haughty sex" to recognize that women's "souls are by nature *equal* to yours." Her feminist vision extended to the ministries of Antoinette Brown Blackwell and Olympia Brown in the nineteenth century and to Shirley Ranck's efforts to restore devotion to the Goddess in the twentieth. Unitarian ministers Theodore Parker and Samuel Joseph May and laywomen Maria Weston Chapman and Lydia Maria Child were among the most fervent abolitionists in the 1840s, their fervor matched by civil rights martyrs James Reeb and Viola Liuzzo in the 1960s. Universalists Charles and John Murray Spear were among the first ministers in the United States to call for an end to the death penalty. Rachel Carson's pioneering environmental activism found an early champion in Supreme Court Justice William Douglas, who also was sustained by a Unitarian Universalist faith. The heritage continues today in examples too numerous to name.

This legacy is not unique, nor is it unmixed. Unitarians may have made great abolitionists; they also made great slave traders. Unitarian and Universalist activists have always had much to learn from the prophetic leaders of other traditions, from the fiery Calvinist John Brown to the peaceful Hindu Mohandas Gandhi.

Therefore, it is not enough to recite a litany of heroic stories. We must also ask, what parts of these stories should be most alive in our congregations today? What is our unique and ongoing contribution to the larger struggle for beloved community, for an end to oppression of all sorts, and for reconciliation with our beautiful and tortured earth?

This contribution can be expressed in the words *sacred fire*. For Unitarians and Universalists, work for social justice *is* sacred. It does not depend on any authoritative book or tradition to make it so. Other activists may claim that a supernatural revelation or direct call from God has impelled them to work for justice, and it is not our place to question their testimony. For us, though, the revelation and holy encounter are not "out there" but right here. To visit a prisoner, build a windmill, assist a fugitive from slavery, to shake off our own literal or metaphorical chains—all these actions connect us to the holy as surely as anything we might do at church. We meet God when we see, touch, and hear others, especially those struggling to affirm their inherent dignity in the face of injustice.

Though Unitarian Universalists have no monopoly on such encounters, we are uniquely positioned to take them seriously, because our religion has always been defined more by our understanding of human nature than of God. William Ellery Channing and other early Unitarians rejected the Calvinist doctrine of original sin and affirmed—along with an ancient Christian tradition—that the real purpose of human life was to grow in likeness to God, revealing ever more fully the inborn *imago dei*, or image of God. In the 1828 essay "Likeness to God," Channing declared, "God becomes a real being to us in proportion as his own nature is unfolded within us."

Channing's theology marked a departure from the history of Christian social reform. Previous reformers typically took God's revealed commandments as their starting point. "Thus saith the Lord," thundered the Hebrew prophet, before launching into a denunciation of the hypocrisy and inequality of his society, and twentieth-century prophets from Dorothy Day to Jim Wallis have echoed this approach. Channing's call for people to nurture their inner divinity inspired a different style of activism—not only for his fellow Unitarians but also for Universalists, Hicksite Quakers, and radicals "coming out" of conventional churches to devote their full energies to social reform. Channing's words were treasured by abolitionists William Lloyd Garrison (a renegade Baptist) and Lucretia Mott (a liberal Quaker) because they made it possible to see God in both the victims of violence and slavery and the activists who struggled against injustice. Their friend Henry Clarke Wright, in *Anthropology*, summed up the implications of Channing's theology when he affirmed that "the science of man is the science of God. . . . I shall no more go out of this world, after [God], while I live in it—but shall commune with [God] by communing with what I find here."

Channing's emphasis on the inner divinity of each person was cherished by the Unitarian founders of the Massachusetts and American Peace Societies. While the historic peace churches had emphasized the New Testament command to turn the other cheek, Noah Worcester, William Ladd, and Adin Ballou placed first emphasis on what they saw as a natural human inclination to peace. "There is nothing in the nature of mankind, which renders war necessary and unavoidable," wrote Worcester in *A Solemn Review of the Custom War*. Ladd anticipated the later anthropology of peace by citing examples of peaceful societies, and Ballou insisted that violence could be unlearned "without annihilating or perverting any essential constituent" of human nature.

Other Universalists and Unitarians moved from human nature to social justice by different paths. The earliest Universalists did not share Channing's confidence in the divinity of human nature, but their conviction that God would save all humanity galvanized a powerful sense of social solidarity. John and Charles Spear reached out to prisoners because they recognized them as fellow recipients of saving grace, and a century later Clarence Skinner extolled the Universalist faith in "the common destiny of humanity."

By Skinner's time, some Unitarians and Universalists believed they could move from human nature to social justice without invoking God at all. "The only religion that can ultimately save," declared the humanist John Dietrich, is "faith in man." For Dietrich, Channing's anthropology could stand without his theology, and in Dietrich's sermon "Unitarianism and Humanism," he spoke out against war and unfair labor practices.

The underlying disagreement between Dietrich and Channing should remind us that our faith in humanity does not require a common theory of human nature. Channing and his Universalist contemporary Hosea Ballou understood the relationship between body and spirit differently, with significant implications for their theologies. The early Unitarians and Transcendentalists claimed that the divinity of human nature is inherent in each individual, while the Universalist theme of universal salvation stressed the solidarity of the whole human race. For many contemporary Unitarian Universalists, our dignity or divinity is grounded not only in our social solidarity but in our participation in the interdependent web of all life. Others might worry that the language of *human dignity* or *human rights* implies an underlying sameness and would insist that the real cause of injustice is our failure to come to terms with radical difference. Ethicist Gabriella Lettini, a non-Unitarian Universalist who teaches at the Starr King School for the Ministry, has made this point especially vigorously, arguing that all Western cultures are infected with an "allergy to the other."

These differences are fascinating, but whether we think in terms of common human nature or radical otherness, of inherent dignity or inherent divinity, we cannot escape the sacred fire lit when we bring our full religious devotion to our encounters with other people. All the abolitionists testified to this, often using the sort of fervent, evangelical language we do not often associate with religious liberalism. William Lloyd Garrison, in his preface to Frederick Douglass's *Narrative*, wrote that when he first met Douglass, he had "never hated slavery so intensely as at that moment," because in the person of Douglass he encountered the "godlike nature" of slavery's victims. Lydia Maria Child was similarly transformed by her literary partnership with the fugitive slave Harriet Jacobs, who used her autobiography to highlight both her victimization and her agency—faced with the sexual brutality of her master, she voluntarily took another white man as her lover and protector. Such testimony challenged Child's assumptions about women's inherent purity, and she in turn wrote numerous stories that challenged her readers to explore the moral choices that enslaved people made in difficult situations.

Our social justice heritage includes dozens of stories like these. Both fleeting and long-standing encounters with other people have fostered lives of commitment. When a bedraggled stranger handed John Haynes Holmes a copy of Henry George's *Progress and Poverty*—a biting denunciation of the prevalence of poverty in prosperous industrial societies—the encounter spurred the novice minister's resolve to transform his class-bound congregation into a true community church, bringing together people of all classes and races.

Holmes also cofounded the National Association for the Advancement of Colored People (NAACP), which quickly became the leading place of encounter between European Americans and African Americans. In this work, he followed the lead of Unitarian women who had built their own antiracist work on a foundation of one-to-one relationships. Celia Parker Woolley and Fannie Barrier Williams—one white, one black, both members of All Souls Unitarian in Chicago—together integrated the Chicago Woman's Club and cofounded one of the first urban settlement houses for African Americans. When Mary White Ovington launched a similar effort in Harlem, she apprenticed herself to a range of black leaders, among them Booker T. Washington, W. E. B. DuBois, and George Simms, pastor of the black Baptist church nearest her settlement. Simms's church, she recalled in her account *Black and White Sat Down Together*, was a place where "newly arrived Southerners" could "get happy" with sermons that were "madly picturesque and yet full of common sense." Simms broke down Ovington's liberal prejudice against the evangelical style by welcoming suffragists to his church and making "the best speech of any." Such relationships were key to founding the NAACP.

In every encounter just described, at least one person involved was neither Unitarian nor Universalist. This fact is of vital importance to our conversation about social justice. If, as I have argued, our Unitarian Universalist faith centers on the religious experience of encounter with other people, then our religious practice must necessarily be one of partnership. The sacred fire that burns among us is not just among Unitarian Universalists—it is inseparable from the interconnected social and ecological web of which we are a small part.

Partnership continues to be integral to most successful Unitarian Universalist social justice ministries, from local living wage campaigns to coalition-based lobbying by the Unitarian Universalist Association Washington Office for Advocacy to the public witness for immigrant rights at the 2009 General Assembly, planned in cooperation with Mormon and Roman Catholic leaders in Salt Lake City. At the same time, the ideal of partnership can and should challenge some of the ways we think about ourselves as a religious movement. Three challenges particularly merit our thoughtful reflection.

The first has to do with congregational polity. As an "Association of Congregations," we value the diverse local expressions of our faith, and rightly so. The sacred encounter between people is inherently local, possible only between particular people in particular places. However, it is not inherently congregational. Community ministries and interfaith justice groups are also local expressions of our faith, and they deserve both financial support and a voice at the national table.

A second challenge has to do with our growth as a religious movement. Increasing our membership is not the only path to a stronger public witness. We can also partner with other faith communities on social justice projects, and have a long history of doing so. Partnering with others can go hand in hand with numerical growth. Both depend on strong habits of hospitality and welcome. Too often, though, our outreach emphasizes our differences from other religious traditions more than our solidarity with them. This tempts us to welcome others only as people who need something that we have and that they can gain only by becoming Unitarian Universalist. If we are serious about the divine potential of human nature, we must also welcome others as people who already possess the sacred fire themselves.

Such a practice of welcome entails a more personal challenge. Because our history is so rich, it is easy for Unitarian Universalists to see ourselves as the ones who already know the path forward to beloved community. Serious partnership requires us to apprentice ourselves, as Mary White Ovington did, to people who might at first seem too different from us to teach us anything. These mentors could be soldiers returning from wars that many of us had protested. They might be former gang leaders, who know what it means to build community under fire. They might be Roman Catholic devotees of the Virgin of Guadalupe, who know how to celebrate beauty in the midst of poverty.

To focus on one example, apprenticeships might transform Unitarian Universalist adoption practices. Many Unitarian Universalists celebrate adoption, particularly transracial adoption, as a profound expression of welcome and as a visible reminder that family comes in many beautiful forms. However, if these public celebrations are not balanced with critical analysis of the adoption industry, they can make our congregations unwelcoming places for parents who have relinquished children to be adopted by others—and for children who still mourn the loss of their first parents. One way to move forward would be for congregational leaders to apprentice themselves to these mothers, fathers, and children, welcoming them not only as "victims" of the adoption system but as people with sacred gifts of love, genetic connectedness, and (in the case of mothers) breast milk. These apprenticeships could empower us to speak out against the policies and institutions that pressure parents to relinquish children because the parents are poor or young or single. They might even inspire us to create more expansive models of family, in which children need not lose their first parents in order to be embraced by a wider circle of caring.

As this example might suggest, the practice of partnership is inescapably risky. In taking those risks, we build on a tradition that can be traced back to Joseph Tuckerman—the man often seen as the founder of Unitarian social justice ministry. When Tuckerman launched his "ministry at large" to Boston's poor in 1826, his first act was to go out and meet the poor, entering "almost tremblingly the houses of the poor where he was a stranger, to offer his sympathy and friendship." He probably believed, paternalistically, that he had more to give to the poor than he had to learn from them, but he put himself in the position of a vulnerable learner. He had recently resigned his pastorate in Chelsea, Massachusetts, because of health problems and a failing voice, and he brought that sense of failure to his meetings with the poor. In "A Discourse on the Life and Character of the Rev. Dr. Tuckerman," his friend William Ellery Channing describes clearly the depth of Tuckerman's transformation: "So deep was the sympathy, so intense the interest, which the poor excited in him, that it seemed as if a new fountain of love had been opened within him."

All of us can open up new fountains of love simply by encountering other people. To do this, we must resist the segregating structures of our society that keep us apart—red states and blue states, class-stratified neighborhoods and suburbs, a school system that divides people rigidly by age, and churches that have scarcely changed their racial and class makeup since the civil rights movement. Those of us who belong to relatively privileged, middle-class congregations must not assume that our churches will be the only or even the primary locations for social transformation. Like Mary White Ovington and Joseph Tuckerman, we must remember that authentic encounters happen more readily in places of struggle than in places of privilege.

It is hard to imagine a better time for the sacred work of encountering others. The recent presidential election revealed that some of the walls that once divided people are crumbling. Many of us thought that working-class whites and Hispanics would not vote for a black president, but they did. Many of us thought that a generation enamored of the Internet would not get involved in doing real-world work to promote the common good, but thousands of young people spent long days knocking on doors and making phone calls. Still, even the most inspiring leader can be only a symbol of the change for which we yearn. The sacred temple in which the fire of divine presence burns brightest is not the White House but every house where strangers break bread together. The priests chosen to light that fire are not presidents or senators but gang members and single mothers and newborn babies. The appointed Sabbath is not election day but every day. May we all have the eyes to see, the ears to hear, and the hearts to burn with holy, human fire.

Powerful Honesty

NANCY McDONALD LADD

In recent decades, the mainline Protestant tradition has suffered what many see as a steady progression toward marginalization and relative powerlessness in social and political spheres. Few would contend that mainline churches are the forces for prophetic change they once were. This shift away from prophetic authority has something important to say to Unitarian Universalists. In the twenty-first century, Unitarian Universalism stands poised either to follow a similarly marginalized path or to move, together with our co-religionists in progressive, mainline, and interfaith spheres, into a phase of power, honesty, and prophecy.

We can chart a course toward the latter destination if we look squarely at the theology and history of the marginalization taking place, explore their significance in our contemporary context, and pay heed to the problem of evil. This work, combined with setting aside our isolationism and exceptionalism, might enable us to join with religious people across a broad spectrum of beliefs to make a difference in the next several decades.

I am a new minister, having graduated from seminary in 2004. Along with many others who joined the ranks of UU clergy in recent years, my ministry had its genesis in the decade of September 11, the Iraq war, Abu Ghraib, Hurricane Katrina, and Darfur. Recently, my congregants in the Washington DC area found themselves cowering in fear of sniper's bullets. In many ways, the sociopolitical backdrop of my ministerial formation has been one of unusually palpable tragedy, confusion, partisanship, and division. We are in a formative period for our faith, ripe for honest healing, even and especially within our most painful contexts. I would not trade the opportunity to minister in these days for anything.

With this tragic sense of contemporary history, my sensibilities are far removed from those that led nineteenth-century Unitarian leader James Freeman Clarke to wed Unitarianism to the notion of "the progress of Mankind, onward and upward forever." Our tradition's insistence on an energizing if oversimplified rhetoric of optimism never seemed as compelling to me as our need to simply be with those in crisis. The work of social justice today entails, first, acknowledging our limitations, our theological weaknesses, and our complicity with political division. The second step is reaching out to partners throughout our religious and secular culture to bring about effective change. We are called not to idealism or optimism but to articulating a theology deep enough to heal, and a theodicy—a system for understanding evil's coexistence with the sacred—that demonstrates our ability to bring about change in this flawed and broken world.

In 2006, Bill Schulz's Berry Street essay "What Torture's Taught Me" challenged the unwillingness among some UUs to directly confront the reality of evil and suffering in this world. If our faith is to be relevant to as searing and profound an issue as torture, we must look unabashedly at humanity's brokenness, from which Unitarians and Universalists have historically shied away. Schulz cites the beloved first principle of the Unitarian Universalist Association—"the inherent worth and dignity of every person"—and our historically optimistic view of human nature as key components of the problem. They suggest that people are inherently good and that evil exists somehow apart from our own best efforts to bring about the good.

At least in part, Schulz's subject is nothing less than the age-old problem of evil—a particularly perplexing issue for us, given our emphasis on human power and perfectibility. Over the last several decades, many scholars have posited that twentieth-century liberal Christianity grievously overestimated human virtue and that this has dealt a debilitating blow to liberal Christian churches. Likewise, in the twenty-first century, it seems that UUs grievously overestimate not only human virtue generally but also our own virtue and power, both as individuals and as part of a small select group.

To understand our predicament, we must tap into the wellsprings from which our beliefs and attitudes emerge: the teachings of mainline and UU social ethicists and theologians such as Walter Raushenbusch, Reinhold Niebuhr, and James Luther Adams, whose theologies contended with two world wars. Their work brought to light the increasing marginalization of the mainline church and sought to address the weakening of the church's prophetic power. Since our understanding springs from their insights, we are not only privy to their wisdom but also vulnerable to their shortcomings.

Walter Raushenbusch helped lead a movement at the beginning of the twentieth century to turn churches away from largely pietistic endeavors toward addressing society's ills. This Social Gospel movement proved a perfect match for the theology and outlook of many liberal religious people at the time, including Unitarians and Universalists.

Raushenbusch and his allies believed that political and social action of people of faith could bring about the kingdom of God on earth. His idea of the kingdom was not apocalyptic but had to do with transforming the social order to fulfill God's vision for it. Social Gospel preachers exhorted churches to partner with God to make manifest in society what was once merely a prophetic vision.

The Social Gospel movement attracted people with political and theological positions ranging from pacifism to socialism, and some Unitarian leaders, such as John Haynes Holmes, found themselves right at home. But, the Great War caused many in the movement to question the practicality and depth of unqualified pacifism. In the face of such brutality, some Social Gospel advocates questioned whether they were living through any human progress at all, despite their myriad efforts to bring about the kingdom. Contrary voices and scathing critiques rose up within the Social Gospel tradition, including radical social ethicists and liberal religionists—our forebears in faith.

No thinker attacked the perceived naïveté of the Social Gospel better than Reinhold Niebuhr. The movement that Niebuhr helped to found and lead, commonly known as Christian Realism, made a powerful mark on the history of religious and social ethics. Generally, Christian Realists hewed closely to the aims of the Social Gospel, but they paired their activism with a firm denial of the progressivist view of history. Social justice work came hand in hand with tragedy, and faith in the unending progress of history was too easily shaken by the realities of twentieth-century struggle. Christian Realists sought a hardier worldview that would not crumble under the reality of suffering. Niebuhr's movement, while politically radical, faced the world's sin and brokenness without flinching. Niebuhr argued that a weakened, sentimental Protestantism could never catalyze the change it celebrated. Pulpit calls to idealistic aims would do little more than push well-intentioned people toward inevitable failure and powerlessness. It was better to acknowledge the world's inherent brokenness and link this with radical social and political concepts that could shape society into its best possible structure.

Niebuhr pursued socialist aims similar to many of his Social Gospel forebears, predicting the downfall of modern capitalism, advocating for more equal distribution of wealth, and decrying all forms of utopianism, including communism. Human evil, to the Christian Realists, most often resulted from hubris, which in turn often resulted from excessive party or group identification. Niebuhr believed that morality might well exist for the individual but seldom if ever held sway for groups. He taught that human evil reigned whenever a group deluded itself enough to believe that its assumptions were absolutely correct.

Of course, not everyone agreed with Niebuhr and his companions. Pacifist Unitarian minister John Haynes Holmes found Niebuhr's approach nothing short of defeatism. Today, even a cursory reading of Niebuhr's life and work reveals his greatest flaw:

the same egotism he adamantly decried. Still, his critique casts a very long shadow over the legacy of the Social Gospel to this day.

Among UUs, no theologian was more widely influenced by the work of Niebuhr and the Christian Realists than James Luther Adams. He argued that until our tradition came to terms with our chronic avoidance of evil and our inability to name sin, we would never truly harness the power to change the world.

In his 1941 Berry Street address, "The Changing Reputation of Human Nature," Adams said, "Certainly, if there is progress, it is not simple configuration of upward trends. At times, it looks more like a thing of shreds and patches. The general tendency of liberalism has been to neglect this tragic factor of history." This tragic sense of history did not commend a cynical and defeatist withdrawal of religion from the sphere of social influence. Rather, it invoked a sense of caution: While religious people must labor for justice, no person or group should naïvely assume that those efforts will prove over time to work wholly for the realization of the good. Adams continued:

> When we say that history is tragic, we mean that the perversions and failures in history are associated precisely with the highest creative powers of humanity and thus with our greatest achievements. . . . The very means and evidences of progress turn out again and again to be also the instruments of perversion or destruction.

As with mainline advocates of Christian Realism, Adams believed the arrogance that accompanies believing one's views to be inherently right is the source of great delusion and even profound evil in this world. The creative powers and sources of progress that keep us going can just as easily bring about the downfall of our ideals.

While Niebuhr focused on the corrupting powers of groupthink, Adams decried the idolization of the individual. He saw many fellow Unitarians assume—as did the Transcendentalists—that speaking from our truest selves would magnify the prophecy and power of our social justice work. Adams pointed out that a group of individuals speaking their separate minds does not constitute a structure of effective social change.

If we pair Adams's critique with that of the Christian Realists, we can conclude that twentieth-century liberal religious social ethics point us away from placing too much faith in either our group affiliation or our individual capacities. Excessive identification with any one group or party can lead to a failure to name and understand that group's weaknesses. At the same time, excessive individualism can lead to a failure to understand one's own faults.

Niebuhr's constant emphasis on the inevitability of failure often comes across as cynical. Yet awareness of our own fallibility is a lesson we would do well to learn. A good dose of humility in the presence of incalculable evil can reinforce our theological grounding and give us the power to be more effective agents of change. When we are overly convinced of our own power and the purity of our message, we do not feel compelled to be part of the larger religious experience. As a result, we marginalize ourselves and drain our power through isolation. Only when we acknowledge our own limitations—when we acknowledge that our assumptions might be wrong, our numbers too small to do all that must be done, our vision too narrow to embrace the whole of our calling—can we come into our potential, by joining with a wider religious community with broader ideas and capacities. We need one another now more than ever, not as self-identified theists or humanists, not as UUs or Christians, not as Democrats or Republicans, but as shared stakeholders in the future.

Many of our personal opinions, and much of the current orthodoxy of our chosen group, will likely prove to be wrong over time. The tasks that are of utmost importance can never be completed by us alone. May these truths be not impediments to change but impetus to change. In place of hubris, let us find a powerful humility, and from the realism born of that humility may we create a radically changed world.

Resisting Evil, Reverencing Life

REBECCA ANN PARKER

Unitarian Universalist social justice work has long been haunted by the notion that theological liberals lack a sufficient understanding of evil. This common critique dates back at least to 1918, when William Wallace Fenn, then dean of the Divinity School at Harvard, bewailed the optimism of religious liberals that blinded them to the human capacity for unspeakable and senseless violence that the horrors of world war had revealed.

Doubts about liberal optimism were answered with the 1933 Humanist Manifesto. This statement asserted the power of the human capacity for good and the promise of progress, especially if God is left out of the equation and human reason, will, and science are brought to the fore. From the mid-twentieth century onward, however, Unitarian theologian James Luther Adams countered these trends, perhaps sensing their kinship with Nazism's white supremacist agenda, which so triumphantly aimed to purge human "imperfection." In the essay "Guiding Principles of a Free Faith," Adams balanced respect for humanity's power with honesty about the human capacity for evil—destructive impulses that "seem veritably to possess people, blinding them, inciting them to greed, damaging the holy gifts God provides." Adams also retained a theological affirmation of transcendent sources of grace and accountability, which some would call God.

More recent generations of theologians and social ethicists

have continued to probe the limits of progress, idealism, and individualism separated from the bonds of covenantal community. Meanwhile, much of liberal religion, at least in UU circles, persists in optimistic idealism that sometimes seems to be running on fumes—hence the need for a conference on the theological basis for UU social action.

It is possible to step off the seesaw that alternates between optimistic religious humanism that can be naïve about evil and penitent Protestant orthodoxy that confesses that "there is no health in us." Instead, a theological stance drawing on the early Christian baptismal process, which trained people for spiritual engagement with evil, can unearth a positive view of human capacity that is integrated with a wise and practical understanding of evil. Such integration is worth reconsidering now, in our own context.

James Baldwin wrote in *The Fire Next Time*, "This is the crime of which I accuse my countrymen . . . that they have destroyed and are destroying hundreds of thousands of lives and do not know it and do not want to know it." In this statement, he identified one of evil's most pernicious forms: willful ignorance.

Those who critique liberal religion for having an inadequate theology of sin and evil are right, if that religion cultivates among the faithful a cloistered experience of the world that closes eyes to injustice, numbs senses to its impacts and horrors, and preserves innocence—as if not knowing and not seeing means one is free from responsibility.

Early Christian baptismal practices intended not to re-create innocence but to prepare people to face evil squarely and resist it effectively. At baptism, converts to Christianity ritually severed their allegiance to the operations of evil and entered into accountable community. Imbued with the Holy Spirit, they were anointed to "be christs" and "to do divine deeds" (as expressed by Cyril of Jerusalem). They prepared for baptism through ritual attunement of the senses to divine beauty embodied in earthly manifestations, learned the benefits and practices of exorcism, and underwent intellectual training. These Christian practices can provide insights into how we, in our time, might use our powers to analyze and resist evil.

Evil wears masks. In the Christian tradition, evil is rarely unveiled or blatant, and resistance to evil requires being able to see through its disguises. Most human beings participate in evil only if they believe they are doing something good. War, for example, masquerades as virtuous action, as protection of one's family or one's country, as meaningful sacrifice, as love and courage and excitement. In truth, war is none of these things. Long ago, Augustine wrote vehemently in *City of God* about war's deception, decrying the Punic Wars:

> Tear off the disguise of wild delusion, and look at the naked deeds: weigh them naked, judge them naked. . . . This war was kindled only in order that there "might sound in languid ears the cry of victory." . . . Away then with these deceitful masks, these deluding whitewashes, that things may be truthfully seen and scrutinized.

The spiritual and intellectual capacity to tear off those "deceitful masks" is necessary to resist evil. In a set of fourth-century baptismal instructions to candidates for entrance into the Christian community, Cyril of Jerusalem emphasizes training the mind for argumentation and analysis so that people would not be easily led astray by ideas or doctrines that appear attractive but serve as a cover for destroying life. Alert, engaged, critical minds are necessary for resisting evil.

Critical thinking alone is not sufficient, however. Most mindsets are shaped relationally—that is, are socially constructed—and cannot be deconstructed by analysis and dissent. People hold fast to the ideas that bind them into relationships with others. Reliable relationships are key to survival in infancy and early childhood, as well as during times of illness and diminished capacity, and they contribute markedly to happiness and well-being throughout life. Humans are neither self-made nor capable of surviving long outside social networks. At our deepest levels, humans need to be known and loved, to be fed and sheltered. These needs deserve respect and attention. Evil exploits them.

For example, pomp and greed play on our human needs for love, recognition, and nourishment. In John Milton's *Paradise Lost*, once banished from the celestial realms, Satan begins his plot to overthrow heaven by creating an ostentatious temple, a huge edifice that rises from the earth, supported by ornate columns and populated by splendidly dressed lesser demons: "devils to adore as deities." Satan's palace, for which the Puritan Milton coined the term *pandemonium*, is an image of the pageantry that helped sustain the unholy alliance of the aristocracy and the church hierarchy that kept many in poverty. Twentieth-century feminist Mary Daly speaks of poisonous processions, decrying the pomp and circumstance that sustain patriarchy. Thandeka, author of another essay in this volume, in her book *Learning to Be White* analyzes why many working poor whites vote against their own economic interest, showing how illusions of economic advancement allow poor whites to define an identity that segregates them from blacks.

This is the way of evil: It parades idols and takes prisoners into its train. Pomp seduces with displays that inflate the worth of some in the public eye, while others are displaced, marked as unworthy, and disdained. Pomp leaves vacancies and deficits in human souls, and it rests on social arrangements that exploit the many in service to the elite few. Its evil lies in the economic, gender, and racial inequities it promulgates without relief and protects with violence.

Evil, operating as fraud, pomp, and greed, manifests as large-scale systems that effectively disrespect and deny basic human needs, disrupt human longings for recognition and connection, exploit resources without replenishment, and maintain social order through treating human beings with violence. Questions such as, Why does evil exist? and, How could a good God create a world with so much evil in it? provide interesting intellectual exercises—but a far more important use of intellectual resources is to see, name, and analyze the presence of evil and its operations.

More important than the *why* are questions such as, What evil is going on here and now? How can it be stopped? How can human beings be liberated from their captivity to it?

If one's primary society or community functions in life-destroying ways, it is possible to dissent, to see through evil's disguises, and to pursue alternative ways of life—but only up to a point. This captivity is vividly clear in modern life with respect to burning carbon fuels. Contemporary market capitalism, with its high reliance on fossil fuels, is arguably evil. It appears to offer a satisfying lifestyle to many, but that well-being—the physical comfort, high quality of food, material wealth of resources that middle- and upper-classes enjoy—is fraudulent. Those of us who experience its benefits do so within a complex global economic system that harms the planet, leaves many in poverty, and threatens the sustainability of life. Fossil fuels are not an isolated example; evil is inescapable in our globalized age. We can see this and can imagine that by seeing and seeking to dissent from it, we are ameliorating harm or resisting evil. However, individuals cannot resist evil on their own. The evil we participate in is transpersonal; it is collective and collaborative. Resisting evil requires collective and collaborative efforts. The social character of evil requires social forms of resistance.

Resisting evil is not about personal escape from guilt, sin, or punishment. It is about ending the harm that evil perpetuates and creating justice and abundance for all. The early Christian church understood the demonic to operate in transpersonal forces that inhabit human beings, surrounding them and holding them captive in a prison that prevents abundant life. The early church performed exorcisms to free the community and its members from the internalized and embedded demons that enabled evil to continue. While talk of demons may sound strange to contemporary, rational people, the religious idea of demon possession is not difficult to apply. Using the example of market capitalism, most of us are inhabited internally and captive externally to its force. It is virtually impossible to escape.

Ritual exorcisms called the names of demons and employed dramatic, symbolic actions in the theater of the gathered community. Exorcisms engaged individuals and the social body in a collaborative effort to identify and subdue life-threatening forces by bringing them under the control of the rational will, expelling them by the power of the spirit, or transforming them through spiritual practice and discipline. The early Christian church performed exorcisms in Jesus' name. New Testament scholar Richard Horsely, in *The Spiral of Violence*, details the ways Jesus' teachings functioned to counteract the destructive policies of Roman imperialism. The ethical teachings of Jesus were strategies for liberation from internalized oppression, and they called people into modes of relational life (mutual care, nonviolence, generosity) that enabled their communities to elude the full weight of domination.

Unitarian Universalism's confidence in human capacity can cloak our vulnerability to our own version of demonic possession. Economically and educationally privileged people can enjoy freedom of speech, freedom of belief, and freedom to determine the course of their own lives and yet remain enmeshed in larger social forces that are harmful to life. The early church called people to name the demons so that human capacities and gifts, strengthened by mingling in community life and undergirded by the power of the spirit, could be harnessed to resist and subdue those forces.

One way ahead for religious humanist and UU social action is to give attention to community life, ritual, and spiritual disciplines through which human capacities and gifts become engaged in resisting evil. Religious life must assist people in observing, analyzing, and becoming wise about evil; its guises, operations, tricks, and habits need to be taught to our children and youth, and faith communities need to commit to engage in ongoing, attentive analysis of its ways. Evil can never be isolated, ever, to something "other" or "out there"; it cannot be seen as something exceptional, present only in the horrible. Evil is so often ordinary, "in here," and pervasive. Evil does not necessarily need to be feared, hated, or destroyed, but it must be stopped. It must not be allowed to cause harm. It has to be interrupted, called out, deflated, disempowered, voted out of office, replaced, redirected, contained, or transformed. Calm clarity and decisiveness in the presence of evil are the marks of spiritual maturity and strength.

Modern religious humanism's and liberal Christianity's anemic response to evil is not due to their celebrating the strength and goodness of human capacities when they should, instead, confess human powerlessness, depravity, and sin. Rather, these traditions have neglected the community life, ritual, and spiritual disciplines through which human capacities become engaged in resisting evil. It is not enough to celebrate "inherent worth and dignity" and assert confidence in the gradual evolution of progress. Religious communities must actively assist healing and recovery from the harm that comes to souls and bodies because of unjust and life-threatening realities. Religious communities must train their members to use their imagination, compassion, creativity, intelligence, conscience, and senses to unmask that which harms life. They must cultivate the rituals and spiritual disciplines that disrupt the hold of the demonic principalities and powers so as to liberate themselves and others from harmful ways of life.

UUs tend to focus on values and ideals as the foundation of social justice work. Striving to walk our talk and build the world we dream about can take individuals and congregations quite far down the path of activism. However, these modes of religious engagement are motivated by something that does not exist: an imaginary better world, a utopia that becomes an imperative, a future possibility that judges the present and demands allegiance. Classically, such activism is rooted in eschatological, prophetic theology. It responds to God's dream of peace and justice, proclaimed by the prophets as the day that will come because God will make it so. Humanity cocreates the kingdom of heaven on earth—or creates it all on its own. Either way, the effort is generated as a striving toward what is not, yet could be. This approach to social justice work rests on a theory of progress—onward and upward forever—that is unwarranted and leads to burnout. In *Saving Paradise*, Rita

Brock and I critique the problems of eschatological imagination as a foundation for justice work. Sharon Welch, another author in this volume, has also raised important objections to it.

For UUs, still singing with gusto that "we'll build a land where we bind up the broken," there is an additional problem. Firm conviction that the Bible is God's word has evaporated. The prophetic proclamations of justice and liberation are no longer regarded as divine promises backed up by divine creativity or the generative present activity of the Holy Spirit. They are merely ideals—lovely visions, dreams, or metaphors. There is no *mysterium tremendum* on which activism rests like a boat running the rapids of justice "cascading down like an ever-flowing stream," as Amos puts it. In the absence of a divine wellspring on which to draw, when the going gets tough, there is nothing to fall back on. Ideals do not administer spiritual assistance; ideals do not come to the kitchen table in the night of fear when a house has been firebombed. Ideals do not surround the soul with comfort or refreshment and renew the heart's courage. For this we need something tangible and alive, something real.

The foundation for social justice work need not be a dream of what could be. It can, instead, be doxology—praise for the gift of life, delight in what we have tasted and seen of beauty, love, tenderness, courage, steadfastness. Grace and gratitude rest in the tangible. Rituals that train the senses to savor the spices, breathe deeply the life-giving air, and be nourished on the feast of wine and bread ground the call to ethical living and justice-making in moments of fullness and sufficiency. This theological perspective links the gifts of life to a life-giving spirit or source larger than ourselves. It attunes people to a spiritual source that impels our striving. This source is not a dream of what should be but a steady wind that fills the sails of our boat.

For the early Christians and now for other communities of resistance, the wind that billows the sails of our life together includes the breath of the spirit of the ancestors, urging the community on. Social action is impelled by "the blessings of the earth and sky," "those who have gone before us," and the "spirit of life" moving in our hands "to give life the shape of justice"—as well as by the cry of those suffering and the haunting silence of the disappeared, the disheartened, and the disinherited. These tangibles are the basis for judgment; they throw the presence of evil into high relief while at the same time provide the impetus to resist evil in whatever guises it presents itself. We are called, as Moses was at the burning bush, to both hear the cries and see the beauty. Thus attuned, we can live a life devoted to liberation and reverence. The first step, as it was for Moses, is to take off our shoes and acknowledge that we are on holy ground.

Audacity, Virtuosity and Wonder

SHARON D. WELCH

In an interview with *Le Monde* in 1980, the French philosopher Michel Foucault gave a poetic invocation of radical social critique:

> I can't help but dream about a kind of criticism that would try not to judge but to bring an oeuvre, a book, a sentence, an idea to life; it would light fires, watch the grass grow, listen to the wind, and catch the sea foam in the breeze and scatter it. It would multiply not judgments but signs of existence; it would summon them, drag them from their sleep. Perhaps it would invent them sometimes—all the better. All the better. Criticism that hands down sentences sends me to sleep; I'd like a criticism of scintillating leaps of the imagination. It would not be sovereign or dressed in red. It would bear the lightning of possible storms.

Foucault's dream is our reality. We find ourselves amidst a third wave of revolutionary politics that builds on two prior waves, yet has its own energy, dynamics, and challenges.

The first wave of revolutionary politics was the forceful denunciation of forms of social injustice: slavery, the oppression of workers, and the secondary status of women—all forms of oppression defended for millennia as divinely ordained or part of the natural order of things. These struggles for justice have been augmented by a second wave of activism: the work of identity politics—the resolute claim for the complex identities and full humanity of all groups marginalized and exploited by systemic oppression, silenced through cultural imperialism, and deprived of cultural respect and full political participation—including people with disabilities; those who are gay, lesbian, bisexual, and/or transgender; and ethnic, racial, and religious minorities.

While the critical work for social justice and human rights goes on, these tasks now occur within a third paradigm of pragmatic political activism. Once we recognize injustice, once we grant the imperative of including the voices and experiences of all peoples, how then do we work together to build just and creative institutions?

I first became aware that the tasks of governing well might differ substantially from the tasks of denouncing and dismantling unjust social systems when I read the *New York Times* obituary of Joe Slovo, a longtime member of the African National Congress who died in 1995. The obituary cited Slovo as saying that nothing in his work in revolutionary politics had prepared him for the challenges of serving as minister of housing in the postapartheid Mandela government. The work of efficiently building equitable housing was formidable, in spite of his commitment to adequate housing for all and his newfound access to the resources necessary to do such work.

Another story that led me to think more critically about the comforting narrative of "us against them on the road to certain victory" lies in the poignant contrast between the *Motorcycle Diaries* and the *Bolivian Diaries* of Che Guevara. The *Motorcycle Diaries* is profoundly moving in its heartfelt depiction of unjust suffering. The *Bolivian Diaries* is profoundly disturbing, written with as much honesty and with as much compassion for people who suffered, yet marked by despair and confusion. At this later point, the revolutionary hero was disenchanted by his failures in the Cuban government as Minister of Industries and alienated by the rejection of the Bolivian communists he sought as allies, who rejected his outsider's thoughts about radical social transformation and governance.

Finally, on a very modest scale, I learned lessons as an academic director of women's studies. Seeing how hard it was for a group of well-intentioned and politically astute radical feminists to run a degree program gave me pause. We found ourselves at odds over required reading lists, faculty appointments, and choices of guest speakers, all matters exacerbated by an inability to engage creatively in conflict. Maybe we were not quite ready to take over the World Bank and other bastions of institutional power.

These three stories have a common thread. To care passionately about justice does not mean knowing how to manage resources creatively and equitably. To thoroughly understand the contours and dynamics of oppression does not imply skill in the task of managing human and natural resources justly, creatively, and sustainably.

This latter task requires a third mode of political engagement. Once we recognize the horrors of injustice, once we foster the full humanity and the differential experiences and histories of all peoples, how then do we work together for social arrangements that are equitable, sustainable, and joyous?

Although it is undoubtedly difficult to live justly and to use power truthfully and well, it is not impossible. The two feminist economists who write together under the name J. K. Gibson-Graham challenge us in *A Postcapitalist Politics* to embrace the intrinsic ambiguity of creating new institutions and to name some of the barriers to such an embrace: "Fearing implication with those in power, we become attached to guarding and demonstrating our purity rather than mucking around in everyday politics." They ask us to follow the guidelines of Eve Sedgwick, recasting our tasks as intellectuals:

> What if we believed, as Sedgwick suggests, that the goal of theory were not only to extend and deepen knowledge by confirming what we already know—that the world is full of cruelty, misery and loss, a place of domination and systemic oppression? What if we asked theory to do some-

thing else—to help us see openings, to help us to find happiness, to provide a space of freedom and possibility?

As an activist, I have seen the impact of speaking truth to power: the inspiration and sense of identity evoked by denunciations of injustice and faithful witness to ideals of justice and peace. In my recent work as a member of the international coalition Global Action to Prevent War, and as a department chair and then a provost, I have been more interested in Sedgwick's challenge. She calls us to use power truthfully as citizens, intellectuals, parents, workers, professionals, and members and leaders of civic organizations to create at least a modicum of justice and peace and flourishing in our communities. We can find a similar focus on using power well in the activism and writing of contemporary Engaged Buddhists.

There are many factors that are important in nurturing and sustaining political engagement. I will focus on two here.

When we see ourselves as embedded, as belonging to this world, a different understanding of the relationship between good and evil emerges. In 1975, working as a research assistant for a church administrator in the months between college and graduate school, I was asked to read and evaluate Mary Daly's *Beyond God the Father*—a devastating indictment of the systemic misogyny of Western religious and philosophical thought. Turning the pages was physically painful. Each new leaf revealed convincing exposition of the ways in which Western Christianity and Western philosophy systematically devalued and denigrated the intelligence and moral capacity of women. I saw the solid support I had received throughout my life from male and female mentors, teachers, and ministers for what it was—a normal openness to the full humanity of women that was, tragically, still all too rare in much of the world. As devastating as it was to acknowledge the depth of misogyny in Western religious traditions, it was equally challenging to ponder the implications of an alternative paradigm, described by Daly in *Beyond God the Father* but never actualized in her work. Once we stop the projection of evil, fallibility, and finitude onto women, we may confront the real mystery and nature of human evil.

There is a story, oft used in leftist politics circles and singularly unhelpful. A man comes to a city and is outraged by the injustice he sees. He stands in the center of the town square and demands justice. At first, a large crowd gathers, but each day, the crowd dwindles until he stands alone—a solitary voice denouncing the evil that continues unabated. One day a passerby asks him, "Why do you speak in the square each day since you are not changing anyone?" He answers, "At first I spoke to change others; now I speak so that they will not change me."

This story places the blame for injustice on the oblivious townspeople and valorizes the bold but ineffectual voice for change. Where can we find another story, one that has the honesty to admit that our failures to change others may well be of our own making? Might *their* recalcitrance and isolation be related to *our* lack of strategic imagination?

The challenge of giving sustainable, material shape to revolutionary aspirations is not served by the isolating rhetoric of righteous indignation, but rather by deep grief at the costs of injustice and a forthright recognition of the failures and limits of the revolutionary vanguard. We need to tell ourselves a new individual and national story, one that forgoes, even for peacemakers, the assumption of moral exceptionalism. Let us consider a set of stories and a type of practice that can enable creativity and wonder in the face of such moral complexity—wisdom drawn from the work of Vietnamese and Japanese Buddhists and Native American writers and activists. Each of these traditions, borne by cultures that the United States tried to defeat militarily and culturally, offers resources for a transformed political and ethical imagination.

In *The Truth About Stories*, Canadian author Thomas King explores the collective identity of indigenous Americans and European Americans. He paints a vivid picture of a guiding narrative of the West: "If we had to have a patron story for North America, we could do worse than the one about Alexander the Great, who, when faced with the puzzle of the Gordian knot, solved that problem with nothing more than a strong arm and a sharp sword."

King juxtaposes this North American image of decisive force with an image clearly expressed within many Native American traditions and, according to King, "overlooked even by sympathetic white readers and interpreters." He reminds us that

> there are other ways of imagining the world, ways that do not depend so much on oppositions as they do on cooperations, and they raise the tantalizing question of what else one might do if confronted with the appearance of evil. So just how would we manage a universe in which the attempt to destroy evil is seen as a form of insanity?

How do we act if we acknowledge that evil is as much within us as it is within our more benighted opponents? How do we act if we also acknowledge the equal power of good and evil? More precisely, how do we act if we acknowledge the equal but *differential* powers of good and evil? Just as evil and force can destroy a social order yet not establish lasting peace, so the good can readily be undone—not only by resentment and fear, but by the dual temptations of self-satisfaction and the use of yesterday's solutions for today's challenges.

We make so many mistakes as activists, as leaders, in our work of cultivating all that is glorious in life. These are due to carelessness, to pettiness, to ill will and ego, to lack of imagination. I have been fortunate in my work with the Laguna Pueblo author and artist Carol Lee Sanchez to learn ways of responding to such mistakes, ways that resonate with my childhood experiences of teasing and honesty at the noontime table on the farm. When I first made a series of disastrous mistakes as director of women's studies, Sanchez stood with me, not denying the gravity of the mistakes but helping me learn from them. She helped me laugh at my own self-righteousness, pride, and ill-conceived stratagems. The wisdom she shared is deeply rooted in the culture and history of her people. In "Landscape, History and the Pueblo Imagination," Leslie Marmon Silko, also from Laguna Pueblo, describes the process of responding to mistakes well with the gift of Laguna storytelling. This oral tradition that recounts "disturbing or provocative" events in the presence of all members of the family, even, and especially, children:

> The effect of these inter-family or inter-clan exchanges is the reassurance of each person that she or he will never be separated or apart from the clan. . . . Neither the worst blunders or disasters nor the greatest financial prosperity and joy will ever be permitted to isolate anyone from the rest of the group. . . . You are never the first to suffer a grave loss or profound humiliation. You are never the first, and you understand that you will probably not be the last to commit or be victimized by a repugnant act.

We are not the first to suffer and fail, and we will not be the last. We are not the first to also embody a measure of justice, and we will not be the last.

I speak today with peacemakers who acknowledge that we really do not know how to bring about peace, reconciliation, and justice. The solutions that seem so promising in theory prove to be surprisingly complex and ambiguous in actuality. However, we remain committed to the art of working for peace and justice for all beings—even as we admit that we do not know how to bring these things to a world of *dukka*, a world of suffering shaped by the poisons of greed, ill will, and delusion. We are learning how to work for justice in this world. Our histories equip us to readily see the fixations of other individuals, peoples, and nations. Our present contexts demand enough honesty and self-awareness that we might catch a glimpse of our own delusions.

Those of us working for peace are not a righteous vanguard. We can, and will, abuse cooperative power and need our own Trickster stories to remind us of our flaws and excesses. There is no multitude, no group any less likely than others to abuse power. Frantz Fanon, a preeminent teacher of the psychopathology of colonization, knew this well, and revolutionaries of all sorts forget this to our peril. Wisdom, ongoing self-critique, and accountability are required of all of us, not just the imperial others, when we exercise social, cultural, economic, and political power.

Our goal is neither the ultimate defeat of evil nor fundamental and permanent social change. It is simply (but significantly) a less destructive way of playing who and what we are. For this, we need new transformative metaphors for compassionate, self-critical, and creative engagement.

The metaphors for our justice work in the past were as evocative as they were partial: "Sisterhood is powerful"; "Workers of the world, unite, you have nothing to lose but your chains"; "A dream deferred is a dream denied"; "Let justice roll like waters, and righteousness like a mighty stream." How do we express most vividly our appeals now—not just to sisterhood and to workers, but to all humanity—for sustainable peace, for enduring security, and for nurtured dreams? This is a complex task, to be sure. But let us be artisans of hope, artisans of wonder, working with the clay of human longing, of our capacities for greed and indifference, exclusion and fear, as well as for generosity, courage, forgiveness, and resilience. Let us build flourishing communities of honesty, inclusion, self-critique, and hope.

What Will We Be and For Whom?

KAT LIU

I first learned about Unitarian Universalism in college from friends planning to get married. They were unenthused about being married by a judge but equally unenthused about having God invoked in their nuptials. They found in Unitarian Universalism the perfect compromise. My friends described Unitarian Universalism as a religion "where you can believe anything you want." While I was happy that such a faith existed to serve their wedding needs, I did not understand why anyone would want to actually join such a "faith." This kind of fluffy, feel-good religion held no appeal for me as a young Chinese-American woman, struggling to navigate between the U.S. American ideal of individual liberty and the Asian ideal of communal responsibility.

Nevertheless, years later, when I moved from my native California to New York, I realized that without friends or community, the social engagement I had thought a natural part of my identity was slipping away in my isolation. I decided to investigate the local Unitarian Universalist congregation. Everyone in the little all-white fellowship was pleasant enough, and I became a sporadic, uncommitted, ambivalent attendee. When new acquaintances asked what my religion was, I uncomfortably responded that I attended a UU fellowship, but I never identified as a UU.

A change of careers took me to Washington DC, and one Sunday I dropped by the local UU congregation. At the introductory session following the service, a newcomer remarked that her favorite aspect of Unitarian Universalism was that you could believe whatever you wanted. I started making plans to be elsewhere the following Sunday. But then the minister gently questioned the statement. "Is that really true?" she asked. "Or is it that you are free to believe what your conscience calls you to believe?" My ears perked up. Over the next two weeks I learned from ministers and congregants about a faith that valued liberty for the sake of justice—individual autonomy balanced with communal accountability. I had known about Unitarian Universalism for two decades without much interest, yet in less than two weeks I enthusiastically signed the membership book.

I had found a home. As an Asian American—particularly one who grew up in a white neighborhood—there were few places where I felt comfortable at the time. In all-white settings I remained acutely aware of my differences, even if others seemed to accept me as one of them. In all-Chinese settings I was often disapprovingly reminded of ways in which I was not fully Chinese. I have come to learn that I am not alone in this regard. For me and many people of color, and even for some Euro-Americans, the settings where we feel most at home are multiracial or multicultural. Amidst a diversity of people, both our similarities and our differences are acknowledged and accepted. Few churches ever attain meaningful ethnic and cultural diversity; fewer still remain that way by deliberately embodying that identity.

Having found a spiritual home after so many years, I became an evangelical UU, eagerly sharing with anyone who would listen my discovery of a justice-seeking religion that not only tolerates diversity but celebrates it. I had no reservations about sharing this good news with people in the local area. However, when talking with people who lived elsewhere, especially people of color, I felt a pang of ambivalence if they voiced interest in investigating Unitarian Universalism. I had told them that my religion celebrates diversity—but what would my friends find when they stepped through the doors of their local house of worship? It was likely that they would see a group less diverse than their own neighborhoods, less diverse than the neighborhood of the church itself. In proclaiming my enthusiasm for Unitarian Universalism as I experienced it in my own congregation, I couldn't help but wonder if I was selling a false bill of goods.

I have also wondered whether Unitarian Universalism is a prophetic religion for our times when it comes to racism and multiculturalism. A prophetic church must lead a community in upholding social justice, which means recognizing the concerns of those at the margins of society and helping to bring those concerns into equal consideration with concerns of those in power. A prophetic religion speaks to its time and community and leads people to a better vision of the future.

By these criteria, one can argue that Unitarianism and Universalism have always been prophetic. Other essays in this volume note our illustrious (and sometimes not so illustrious) past on abolitionism, women's suffrage, and the civil rights movement. Unitarian Universalism recognizes and promotes equality for gay, lesbian, bisexual, and transgender people, sometimes finding itself one of very few religious voices speaking for transgender people. When I think of our work in this area, I am proud to be a UU.

However, much as we cite the work of our religious ancestors on abolition and civil rights, I am less sure of our current commitment to antiracism and multiculturalism. The United States has become increasingly diverse, yet our faith communities remain predominantly white. If we are the prophetic church we claim to be, how can we remain content with congregations less diverse than our neighborhoods? During the last presidential campaign, while UUs praised Obama for the diversity of his supporters and denigrated McCain because he attracted supporters who are mostly whiter of skin and hair, it did not go unnoticed that our UU congregations look far more like McCain's crowd than Obama's.

In the Jewish and Christian roots of our faith, the role of the prophet is to speak truth to power, often through holding governments accountable to a higher standard. Yet today, given the savvy ways the Obama administration has reached out to a wide array of cultural constituencies, it seems that our government is far ahead of our churches. We are not leading; we are not even keeping up. With regard to racial and cultural diversity, we are lagging behind, in danger of becoming irrelevant.

Unitarian Universalism appears to have a generally tepid appeal among people of color. Perhaps one reason for this is our being stuck an Enlightenment or modernist mind-set. Unitarianism was born of the same Enlightenment ideals of reason and tolerance encoded in our nation's foundational documents—noble ideals born from the cultured musings of wealthy white men who saw the strengths of these philosophies without noticing the classist, racist, and sexist views latent within them. The early Unitarian vision of self-cultivation through study and reflection presupposes a person with ample leisure and resources. The watchword *liberty* asserts individualism more prominently than community, and it assumes opportunities that are not always present. While Unitarians promoted tolerance of diverse views, they also believed that judicious application of reason would eventually reveal one objective truth—a viewpoint prophetic and liberating for that modern era, but often dangerous and repressive in postmodern times.

Postmodernism need not only refer to convoluted interpretations of abstract theories by obscure authors. In this context, it means the view that socially, spiritually, ethically, and ethnically, there is no one objectively true reality, but rather multiple subjectively true realities for different people from different perspectives. Thus, in the postmodernist view, diversity is inherently valued, not just added on to a presumed norm. Postmodernism also recognizes that the ideals that are liberating for you may be oppressive to me. For example, "You can believe whatever you want" may be liberating to those who are fleeing the rigid dogmas of some religions, but the same statement is irrelevant and off-putting for others. People who live at the margins of society and are subject to the whims of those in power know that beliefs have serious consequences. Advertising campaigns along the lines of "When in prayer, doubt" may be very appealing to a class of people whose circumstances afford them the time to ponder, but the same phrase is irrelevant and nonsensical to those for whom prayer is the only hope remaining.

Most of our outreach advertises values that appeal predominantly to white, middle-class sensibilities, yet we wonder why it is predominantly white, middle-class visitors who come through our doors, and why the few people of color who make their way to us often leave.

Some people have argued that Unitarian Universalism is not for everyone, that we cannot be all things to all people. While this is true, the question remains—What, then, will we be, and for whom? If we want to be a religion of the race and class privileged, then we need not change, and we can watch society pass us by. If it is our desire to be prophetic leaders in building a multiethnic, multicultural beloved community, we must step outside our culture-bound viewpoints, recognize that other equally valid viewpoints exist, and intentionally work to see through the eyes of others. Those among us who live on various margins have already had to learn to do this.

May we lead, not lag. May we reclaim the voice of our prophetic faith.

Dancing in the Streets

ROBERT M. HARDIES

Historians of the Middle Ages note a curious phenomenon of that otherwise lackluster period of history. The people of Europe would often festoon themselves in masks and costumes, grab their musical instruments, and break into ecstatic fits of communal dancing. These so-called dance manias fill the historical record. In Utrecht, the Netherlands, two hundred people danced so furiously on a bridge that it collapsed, dumping them all into the river. In Italy, fits of spontaneous leg-shaking were blamed on the bite of the tarantula—hence the name of a dance, the tarantella. Naturally, the powers that be frowned upon such fits of collective pleasure and strength, and sometime during the sixteenth century the phenomenon died out.

Barbara Ehrenreich traces the genealogy of ecstatic celebration in her book *Dancing in the Streets*. She argues that a primal intuition drives these dances, still present in cultures across the globe. We dance together because we need each other. Dancing simultaneously expresses and fulfills that need. That is why it gives us joy.

Maybe this explains why my companions and I felt a gravitational pull to the streets of Washington DC at about 11 p.m. on election night 2008. When CNN first called the election for Obama, someone in our party threw open the windows to our apartment; shouts and blaring horns poured in on the night air.

After the speeches were over, we put on our coats and followed the noise all the way to the intersection of 14th and U streets, which police had closed to traffic.

There, a circle of drummers formed the epicenter of a pulsing mosh pit of revelers. Students from Howard University danced on bus shelter roofs and homeless people banged on cans. Fancy dressers from the night clubs danced with progressive hipsters from the Busboys and Poets cafe. There were gay folks and straight, young folks and old. All of us, strangers and friends, high-fiving, fist-bumping, and hugging each other. A singing, dancing, beautiful mass of humanity, one that was replicated on streets across this city, in cities across this nation, and indeed across the world—even in the small Kenyan village where Barack Obama's father was born. Dancing in the streets: an expression of collective joy and solidarity.

Our election night rave at the corner of 14th and U streets vividly evoked for me two other moments in the last half century of American history. As I danced that night, I couldn't shake those resonances from my mind. They have helped me frame my understanding of the meaning of the political moment that we found ourselves in as we inaugurated our nation's first African-American president.

The most visceral of these memories took me by surprise because it seemed entirely incongruous. As I danced with my neighbors in the streets, I could not stop thinking about September 11, 2001. As the memory persisted I realized that was the last time that I saw the people of my city—my nation—treat one another with such tenderness, compassion, and respect. It was last time I had felt such a palpable sense of solidarity and common purpose with my fellow citizens, and the last time I had felt the world offer its warm wishes to our nation.

As I danced, I began to shed tears—tears of regret for how, in the wake of 9/11, we betrayed those brief moments of tenderness and solidarity. How our unity turned to division as terrorism became a wedge driven between red and blue America. How our respect for one another morphed into distrust of Muslims and fear of immigrants. How we went from painstakingly recovering dead bodies from the rubble of the World Trade Center to torturing live bodies in the cells of Abu Ghraib. How our sense of solidarity as US citizens was mocked by the unconscionable response to Hurricane Katrina. How we squandered relationships with friend and foe alike through a preemptive, unnecessary, and unilateral war in Iraq. Even writing this down brings me to tears again.

I still look back and wonder what more we could have done to stop these travesties. As easy as it is to point fingers at others, especially at our political leadership, my tears for this betrayal are, in part, born of guilt and penance. In a democracy, each citizen bears part of the responsibility for the sins of the nation.

One of the things that I hope this election will come to represent is an end of our citizenry's betrayal. For me, that pulsing election night mosh pit felt like a communal exorcism of the demons of 9/11 and a return to the better angels of our nature that we had so briefly embraced in the wake of those attacks.

But the dance is only the beginning. We must all work to atone for the sins of our nation. We must hold our elected leaders accountable for restoring the civil liberties that were taken away, for striking torture once and for all from our legal code, for providing restorative justice to the people of New Orleans, for ending the unjust war in Iraq, and for once again reaching out with an open hand to the rest of the world. Years from now, when we look back on how we used this moment, I want us to be able to say that we brought an end to the long nightmare begun on September 11, 2001.

The dance has another historical resonance. In 1968, in the wake of Dr. King's assassination, an angry riot with its epicenter at the corner of 14th and U destroyed an entire neighborhood, leaving a scar on the city that lasted until the neighborhood was finally redeveloped this past decade. Although the physical infrastructure has been restored, the emotional scars endure to this day. To stand on a street corner destroyed forty years earlier by riotous despair and see instead people of all ages and races dancing with joy filled me with a great sense of hope, a sense that at least some part of a forty-year wilderness journey has finally come to an end. There is no place in the world I would rather have been on election night than on that corner.

Yet the dance is only the beginning. Some members of All Souls Church, Unitarian, in Washington DC, still remember coming to church on the Sunday after the 1968 riots. They remember the smoke that hovered in the air and the layer of dust and debris covering everything. They remember walking past National Guard tanks parked across the street. And they remember the question on everyone's mind: "Where do we go from here?"

In response to that moment, the members of All Souls Church did an extraordinary thing. They led. They hired David Eaton to serve as their first African-American senior minister. Under David's leadership, All Souls grew into a truly multiracial congregation and became one of the few places in the entire city where black folks and white folks could come together to talk and begin rebuilding the community. The church became a center of peace and of opposition to the Vietnam War. Long before Target and Whole Foods came along, back when no one wanted to touch the decimated 14th Street, All Souls was one of the first developers on that ravaged strip, building four hundred units of affordable housing that stand to this day. The church responded to its moment in history and became a leader.

I believe with all my heart that Unitarian Universalism has a leadership role to play at this historic moment. This election was about more than a change in president or party. It represents the renewal of an old dream in America. A dream the founders expressed with the words *E pluribus unum*—out of many, one. *E pluribus unum* may be America's civic religion, but it also expresses a more profound hope lodged deep within the human spirit, expressed by all our religious traditions. Christians call it atonement, *at-one-ment*. Jews call it *tikkun olam*. Dr. King called it the beloved community. At my church we call it, simply, All Souls. It is a vision of the human family—of all creation—reconciled and whole.

This is the dream that got us up and dancing on election night. We dance because we need each other. Dancing is simultaneously the expression of and fulfillment of that need. But the dance is only the beginning. We know we will not achieve this dream by dancing in the streets together, or by electing a black man president of the United States. To achieve this dream, communities all across this nation—congregations foremost among them—must commit and fortify themselves to make the dream a reality, to serve as laboratories, as incubators, of this dream of the human family, reconciled and whole. We must be communities where the divisions that separate us in our daily lives come tumbling down and we recognize ourselves as part of one human family.

William Ellery Channing spoke to this dream when he uttered his famous affirmation, "I am a living member of the great family of all souls." Grounded in his theological affirmation, may we build congregations committed to bearing witness to the human family, reconciled and whole—intentionally multiracial and multicultural churches, theologically pluralistic churches, churches of gay and straight, young and old. If Unitarian Universalist congregations cannot lead us toward that reconciled vision of the human family, who can?

We have a long way to go. On the day after the election, I met with a group of Unitarian Universalist colleagues. We reflected on the scenes of the previous night, including the difference between the crowd gathered at Grant Park for the Obama victory —which was large, young, and diverse—and the McCain crowd— which was smaller, gray-haired, and almost entirely white. Like many others, we snickered at the difference between the two. But later the smiles vanished from our faces when someone noted that most of the congregations in our movement—indeed, most of the congregations of liberal Protestantism—look more like McCain's rally than Obama's. Unitarian Universalists rallied around the Obama campaign with a spiritual fervor, eagerly considering ourselves part of "generation Obama," yet our religious communities currently reflect a different reality.

This is an exciting time to be an American. It is an exciting time to be a Unitarian Universalist. I, for one, am with Emma Goldman, who said, to paraphrase, "I don't want to be part of a revolution that doesn't dance." On election night we had our dance. The dance is only the beginning. Now let's bring on the revolution.

The Urgency of This Moment

ADAM G. GERHARDSTEIN

Prophetic churches minister to the community as it is while reminding the community of what it could be. They transform the community with a vision embodying our Unitarian Universalist principles. Grounded in the here and now, prophetic churches connect this moment with eternity. They reference the past but refuse to conflate it with the present. They forge a vital understanding in congregants: Our present actions help shape the future.

Prophetic churches convey the urgency of this very moment. Too often churches interpret a moment through the layers of history preceding it. While it is important to embrace the contributions of this faith's founders—the abolitionists, the civil rights heroes, and others—to be prophetic we must minister to the struggles in front of our very faces, struggles that our forebears were never given a chance to confront. Prophets of old can never be prophets today; only we can. Our message is most prophetic not when it focuses on how far we have come or how far we have to go, but on where we are now, and how the now connects with the eternal human experience. Our message must be, "Look around you! Grab the hand of your neighbor—*this* is the defining moment!"

I am twenty-six years old. My generation is living in the most multicultural society the world has ever seen—not only globally but in many cases locally. I grew up across the street from an interracial couple and their family; next to them was a large family of

Jamaican immigrants. On one side of my house was a white Appalachian family, on the other, an African-American family. A gay couple lived down the street, next door to Mennonite and Jehovah's Witness families. This setting might not surprise you if I had grown up in New York City—but I didn't. I grew up in Cincinnati, Ohio.

The public schools I attended drew students from every neighborhood in the city, and the youth group at First Unitarian Church of Cincinnati attracted diverse participants engaged in diverse curricula. Like many in my generation, throughout my childhood I floated among cultures, listening to hip-hop and country, watching TV shows about white yuppies in Manhattan and African-American hipsters in Detroit, reading books about the lives of Chinese-American women and black empowerment leaders, attending bar mitzvahs and masses. During my travels as a young adult, I grew to admire other countries' cultures and customs and learned that as multicultural as my life has been, the journey is only beginning. Just by hanging out with my neighbors, classmates, and youth group—and learning of others' lives through literature, worship, film, music, theater, television, and travel—I developed a broad sense of who "my people" truly are.

Millions of young voters like me helped propel Barack Obama to the presidency because we were thrilled to finally find a leader who spoke to the realities of our lives and understood the world in which we live. I personally knocked on hundreds of doors, not only to elect Obama but to reconcile the core of my being with the direction of my country. When I was recently asked, "How does your faith support your justice work?" I immediately responded, "I don't see a difference between the two." My sense of self, belief in God, and commitment to justice all grow out of the multicultural community that has surrounded me my entire life. Respect for "the inherent worth and dignity of every person" is not something I have consciously chosen as a statement of belief; it rests at the core of who I am. When I become aware of sexist, racist, homophobic, or any other type of unjust system, institution, or relationship, I resist. As a member of a multicultural generation,

I have a multicultural expectation. For a ministry to be prophetic today, first and foremost it must have a multicultural expectation.

Prophetic ministry must connect this multicultural moment with the most profound depths of human experience. This can be done at any moment, if we minister to what is right before our eyes. For example, when I served as a legislative assistant in the Unitarian Universalist Association's Washington Office for Advocacy, Rev. Alida DeCoster led my colleagues and me in weekly theological reflection and met with us on an individual basis to tend our pastoral needs. During one such individual session, I shared that a family member was ill, my own health was slipping, my plate overflowed at work, and I was disheartened by initiatives of the Bush administration. After I poured out these stresses, Alida asked simply, "Can I pray for you?"

We held hands, I bowed my head, and she lifted me up in prayer. It was a prayer for strength and courage. She summoned the spirits of love and guidance. In the midst of that storm, she named many blessings and recognized them with gratitude. It was not an eloquent prayer, but it was the perfect prayer. Her prayer nurtured my spirit by offering me exactly what I needed to navigate through the haze, calling out components of human existence that have empowered and sustained us for generations. The prayer was prophetic in that specific moment because it embraced me where I was and took me to a deeper communion with our shared human experience.

Despite such moments of distress, I see no signs of what I have heard referred to as "social justice burnout." Rebecca Parker observes in this volume that when people's work for social justice is motivated by goals such as justice, equality, or peace, the failure to reach these goals can lead to disappointment and fatigue. I feel largely inoculated from this phenomenon because my social justice work is motivated by a commitment to my multicultural community. This community is a source of continual sustenance, camaraderie, feedback, and inspiration to me and my Unitarian Universalist peers. Each step we take toward justice brings us into greater community with people who are facing injustice or working passionately to confront it. Working with such an amazing, life-giving community only leaves us hungry for more work to do.

Unfortunately, my fellow Unitarian Universalist young justice-seekers do not often find such a community in our churches. This is not about a lack of observable diversity in many of our churches. I and young people like me do not necessarily need churches that look like us, but we absolutely need churches that minister to us. Paula Cole Jones's essay in this volume sums up the significant shifts in culture, demographics, opportunities, politics, and technology over the last few decades, claiming that we are living in a new paradigm. My generation knows nothing but this new paradigm. As a movement, if we are going to invite my generation into our churches, we have to make room for it in our pews. This may mean that some people are going to leave—not because we would force them out, but because they are unable to adapt to the new paradigm. To change the way we minister, we have to see these shifts in the pews as a passing of the torch. We are swiftly moving into a new way of thinking and acting—those of us who lead the transition need that torch to light our way, because these paths have not been trod before.

Prophetic ministry seizes the moment with a firm grip, refusing to let the significance of daily existence and shared community slip through our fingers. Prophetic ministry reminds us that at the beginning and end of every day, we are each members of the great family of all souls. Prophetic ministry holds up the kinship and common destiny that we share as a human family, even as it acknowledges our differences. The prophetic church saves our souls while we work to save our world—today.

Healing Souls, Healing a Nation

THANDEKA

Several years ago, I attended the Sunday morning worship service of an evangelical Unitarian Universalist mission in a blighted inner-city community in Roxbury, Massachusetts. While attending a Boston meeting of Unitarian Universalist clergy earlier that week, another minister and I had decided to learn more about the work of a newly credentialed minister who wanted to combine her passion for social justice work with mission outreach. She had planted the message of our liberal faith into the heart of a drug-ridden, desperately poor, HIV/AIDS-riven black and brown Roxbury community.

When my friend and I arrived at the church, although the service had not yet begun the small sanctuary was packed to overflowing with the dispossessed and downtrodden. The weary eyes, pockmarked faces, desperately threadbare and faded clothing, the dirty and unkempt hair of countless congregant street people—all these and more were sure signs that the minister of this church was attempting to practice what we preach: a ministry of inclusion. The music rocked with the evangelical Christian spirit of the minister's own traditional religious background. Toward the middle of the service, there was an altar call.

Raised Baptist, I knew this age-old rite of calling congregants forward to say a few words to the minister and receive in response a personal prayer and blessing. The congregants lined up, waiting quietly and patiently. The line slowly snaked forward as the music continued. Everyone sang. Each person in the line had a chance to whisper something into the minister's ear. Each person then received a personal blessing and then, aglow, rejoined the larger congregation. This ritual lasted for perhaps half an hour.

As my friend and I left the church after the two-hour service and the community meal that followed it, we both wanted to talk about the altar call we had witnessed. "What do you think would happen if we initiated such a ritual in our mainstream Unitarian Universalist congregations?" I asked my friend, who was minister of one of our larger and more prestigious churches.

Whimsical delight flitted across his face. Smiling, he leaned over to me and said in a hushed voice, "Here's what would happen in my congregation. Everyone would line up. The first person would whisper into my ear: 'After the service, I want to talk with you about your sermon.'"

Mission work is not our strongest suit as an association of liberal and progressive congregations. We find it easier to talk about our well-reasoned ideas than to delve into the feelings of our own hearts and enter into the shadowed valleys of our own fears and despair.

Religious evangelicals do not have this problem. They traverse this difficult course into the human heart regularly. They attend to the emotional pain of broken souls. This is why they are so popular. They have leveraged the present collapse of America's economy into their own bull market. They do not turn away from emotional pain—they transform it.

Monsignor Thomas McSweeney, a columnist for Catholic publications and a religion consultant for MSNBC, makes this point when offering advice to traditional Christian pastors. "Today a pastor must set aside the prescribed liturgical calendar and directly address the anxiety in the air [saying] 'I know a lot of you are feeling pain today . . . and we're going to do something about that.'" Right now. Right here. These pastors are saying, Fear be gone. God step in.

Seventh Day Adventist televangelist Don MacKintosh tells us why evangelists can do this kind of transformative work so well.

The *New York Times* quotes him as saying, "Every Christian revival in this country's history has come off a period of rampant greed and fear. That's what we're in today—the time of greed and fear." Evangelists are leveraging pain into spiritual gain. They grab hold of the pain in the human heart and help it find immediate relief.

This is the evangelicals' mission work. It is also our mission work—and our social justice work. A case study demonstrates why.

On December 28, 2008, a front-page headline in the *New York Times* read, "Saying Yes to Anyone, WaMu Built Empire on Shaky Loans." The article begins with focused attention on John D. Parsons, a supervisor at a Washington Mutual mortgage processing center who rarely allowed his employees to question the claims by prospective clients that they had six-figure incomes and more. When regular people—Jack the pipefitter and Jill the secretary—started showing up and declaring their financial wealth in six-figure terms, their claims were accepted at face value. Babysitters, schoolteachers, and landscapers, according to their self-declarations, made as much money as Wall Street brokers, computer wizards in the dot-com world, and national sports figures. Clearly, the only criterion for getting a mortgage loan from Washington Mutual was showing up. As one appraiser put it, "If you were alive, they would give you a loan. Actually, I think if you were dead, they would still give you a loan." Mass media advertising campaigns featured the theme "The power of yes," which, as the reporters note, was also the mantra of the bank employees.

The *Times* chose WaMu for the article's focus because it represented "a singularly brazen case of lax lending." The value of its bad loans, by the first half of last year, had reached $11.5 billion. The system worked because everybody was put on the take. Agents were pressed to disregard borrowers' incomes and pump out loans, and mortgage brokers were given handsome commissions for selling the riskiest loans. Real estate agents were being paid fees over $10,000 to bring in borrowers. Property appraisers were pressured to turn in inflated property values. Employees were forced to sell people loans. (Those who fell behind in the office in Tampa, Florida, were ordered to drive to a WaMu office in Sarasota, an hour away. There they sat in a phone bank with twenty other people, calling customers to push home equity loans.) Borrowers were allowed to set their own range for initial payments, leading eventually to large balloon payments. Top executives were paid bonuses that were not linked to the mortgage losses; between 2001 and 2007, the chief executive officer earned $88 million. These explanations begin to reveal the terror, the emotional intimidation, the threats, and the outright despair that gripped those involved.

WaMu was brought down by repeated blows to the emotional integrity of the human heart. One employee explained that if she dared to approach loan officers to do a more thorough background check on a loan applicant, "they would be furious. . . . They would put it on you, that they weren't going to get paid if you stood in the way." When the employee complained to the supervisor that she no longer wanted to work for the loan officer because she had been yelled at, the supervisor simply responded, "Too bad." So the employee hunkered down in the killing fields of her own emotional integrity. The rule here was, survive. Get the job done. Period. The system emotionally broke almost everyone it touched. The emotional fallout produced shock and massive denial, shame and inordinate feelings of disgrace, or new personal systems of abuse.

The first two kinds of reactions are documented in the *Times* article after the purchase of Washington Mutual for $1.9 billion in September by JP Morgan, followed by the receiving a few weeks later of $25 billion in taxpayer bailout money.

First, the outsiders said they were shocked. As the president of one investment company put it:

> I never had a clue about the amount of off-the-cliff activity that was going on at Washington Mutual, and I was in constant contact with the company. . . . There were people at [Washington Mutual] that orchestrated nothing more than a sham or charade. These people broke every fundamental rule of running a company.

Second, the insiders said their own actions were a disgrace. As one of the employees said, in reflection, "We were giving loans to people that never should have had the loans. . . . We were told from above that that's not our concern. . . . Our concern is just to write the loan."

The *Times* article gives us a graphic sense of the personal cost. The first interview takes place in a prison. A former Washington Mutual employee is serving sixteen months for theft after his fourth drug arrest. His job had been overseeing a team screening mortgage applications. He was the one who said, "Too bad," when an employee turned to him for relief from her ranting boss. How did he maintain his hard edge? He snorted methamphetamines daily. His drug paraphernalia was on clear display on his desk. Everyone saw it. As one employee put it, "Everyone said, 'He gets the job done.'"

We do not have to stretch our imagination any further than our own lives to figure out how some of those employees and outside agents might have survived the repeated blows to their emotional integrity—the kind of blows required to make them do what disgusted them. To get and keep the train of mortgage debt rolling on time, some of them probably drank too much, shopped too much, did legal and illegal drugs, watched TV incessantly, ate too much, went silent at home, or ranted and raved at their partners and kids—and thus they passed their trauma on to the people in their private lives. The trauma born of their workplace was borne home.

We know these stories; they are our own. We, Unitarian Universalists, are these people. There, with the grace of God, are we. If we are working in today's marketplace, chances are we are experiencing repeated blows to the integrity of our own emotional lives. If your company gets downsized, chances are you are doing the work of two or more people who have been let go. If we are teaching or practicing a profession, we witness daily the collapse of a network of social support systems.

We are middle America, and as middle America, we are in pain. Our emotional lives are shattered.

Attention to the emotional abuse entailed in the current economic collapse reveals the theological foundation of our mission work—feeling. As nineteenth-century Unitarian Transcendentalist Margaret Fuller reminds us, "What is done here at home in my heart is my religion." We do not *think* our way home to the heart of our religious faith. We are moved there by emotions, affections, moods, dispositions, and attitudes that have been transformed into personal experiences of regeneration and renewal. This is why we say that personal experience is the first reference for our faith. We feel transformed, reengaged, and enlivened not by a creed or a doctrine but by a heartfelt experience. What occurs here at home in our heart is a foundational experience of our liberal religious tradition.

Twentieth-century religious educator Sophia Lyon Fahs tried to remind us of this affective foundational fact of our liberal faith tradition. In *Why Teach Religion in an Age of Science?* she notes, "The emotional impulses that urge [human]kind to be religious are a part of human nature everywhere and . . . always. We truly need to be religious." We need to be religious because we are emotional souls.

Our emotions and intellect guide, direct, and prioritize our personal religious beliefs, spiritual lives, and moral values. This means that the foundation of our theological work is mission work—mission work to the human heart. We must attend to the ways in which human emotions are treated because they are a foundational building block of our liberal religious faith tradition.

The evil that most of us do in the workplace and in our home life is prompted by blows to our feelings of compassion and empathy, blows to the network of sentiments that create emotional integrity. There is a chokehold on our hearts. We must break that grip; that is our mission work.

Our challenge is to begin this mission work to the human heart while we ourselves are emotionally broken. We must turn to our own religious communities for assistance. We cannot do this work alone because human salvation is not a solo act.

Remember that music moves us. We can add more music to our Sunday services. We can sing favorite hymns such as "Spirit of Life" a cappella, so that the musical pacing is determined by the mood and feelings of the gathered congregation. We can extend musical meditations and interludes, so that the music touches our souls, heals and transforms our feelings.

Remember that prayerful meditations take us into the heart of our own feelings. We can make more time for these extended nonverbal reflections in our Sunday services. These rituals will fill us with a spiritual power greater than ourselves alone. The sacred space created by the gathered community will heal us.

Remember that sermons transport feelings. Our ministers can pay more empathetic attention to the feelings of their congregants. We can say to our gathered community, "I know you are filled with anxiety. We are going to work on that this morning. Spirit of Life, come unto me, come unto you, and bring us peace."

Remember that small-group ministries combine mission and social justice work. These groups meet twice a month so that members can "hear each other into speech," to use the phrase of theologian Nelle Morton, and to work on group projects in service to the wider community. Evangelical churches thrive because of small groups, and we can too.

We are a liberal religious people because we make space for the emotional integrity of the heart as well as the intellectual integrity of the mind. We mend souls, and when we have done so, we move on to the conditions in the workplace that break these souls.

Attention to the emotional issues behind the economic collapse reveals a theological foundation of our social justice work—protecting souls. We must work to stop the emotional abuse that creates human souls who not only participate in their own personal demise but facilitate the economic collapse of our nation. This is social justice work because we strive to alter workplace conditions and the wider social and political contexts that produce broken souls. We work to stop the assault.

We know that broken souls cannot heal our nation. Liberated, healing souls can. When we stay the course, our mission and social justice work together will heal souls and transform us all.

Reimagining the American Dream

MARILYN SEWELL

Early settlers risked life and limb to come to this land—a land strange and unknown to them, but full of promise. These early settlers had a dream. Granted, not all people fell under the purview of the dream—women did not, slaves did not, men who did not own property did not, Native Americans did not. However, once the seed of this dream germinated, its scope expanded as it gained traction. From the very first, the dream included freedom of worship for those who had learned to worship in secret, access to prosperity for those willing to work hard, the possibility of owning land for those who had previously been landless, and escape from society's rigid class boundaries for those whose lives had been locked into place by rank and birth order.

Just as this dream promised much from the very start, it was originally understood to be grounded in holy covenant, with God and with one another. In the words of Governor John Winthrop of Massachusetts, given even before his people disembarked from their ship:

> We are entered into Covenant with [God] for this work. We have taken out a commission. . . . We must be knit together, in this work, as one man. We must entertain each other in brotherly affection. We must be willing to abridge ourselves of our superfluities, for the supply of other's

> necessities. . . . For we must consider that we shall be as a city upon a hill. The eyes of all people are upon us.

This was an amazing dream, further articulated and refined in a document that came some 140 years later, a document that made the heretofore unimaginable claims "that all men are created equal, that they are endowed by their Creator with certain inalienable rights." All men have precisely the same rights? Unheard of! This was the seed of the settlers' American dream taking root. However, as it grew over the decades that followed—even as it expanded to include more people within its boundaries—it was shaken and changed, with much of value distorted or lost along the way.

We are a nation in which freedom is now interpreted to mean that the strong do not have to care for the weak. We are a nation that stinks from corruption at the top, a nation that dresses itself in God language while pandering unashamedly to the rich while ignoring the poor. We are a nation hated and reviled by many other nations and grudgingly tolerated by those who would count us as friends. We are far from being that city upon a hill, that moral compass for other nations—rather, we have decided to build an empire, that a few might flourish at the expense of the many.

Now, with our economy in shambles, with greed and corruption so apparent to all, we have finally awakened to the hard truth that easy money helped us avoid for so long: The economic system we thought was structurally sound turned out to be a house of cards—a chimera based on false premises and inflated profit sheets. The good news is that we have come to a point of reckoning that carries with it the possibility of radical change. I say "radical change" because *radical* means "from the root," and radical change is necessary when no amount of shifting or tweaking will do, when there is no solid core. The change required includes a spiritual dimension, for our country's financial problems are rooted not so much in economic malfeasance as in spiritual decadence.

We have come to understand that the story by which we have lived, the primary cultural narrative, is defunct. I refer to the cultural story of the nation, ostensibly about bringing freedom and democracy to all the world but in truth about building empire. However, I am also referring to the cultural story for the individual, that which defines middle-class goals and aspirations. That story is all about competition and gain. It goes something like this: You work on your resume, starting about age 2 or 3, get into a good elementary school, a good high school, and a good university, where you will make the right connections. You graduate, get a good job, get married, buy a nice house, have 2.3 children, work hard and consume a lot (i.e., buy a lot of toys), get old, and die.

This is not a dream worthy of our lives. The emptiness of it is becoming apparent as young people struggle to find meaning in a society in which their parents serve an economic system that no longer serves them, a system no longer grounded in communal and spiritual values. There is no bailing out a system that is not grounded in relationship, that is bereft of moral principle. We have to build from the bottom up, on new ground and new premises.

Economics is fundamentally a moral discipline. Economics defines our material relationships with one another—Who gets which of society's resources? And it defines our relationship with the natural environment—What are we extracting from Mother Earth, and for what purposes? When we tell a young child, "You have to learn to share," that's economics, and when we say to a two-year-old, "Let's recycle that juice box," that's economics.

The problem with economics as it is treated academically and in the business world is that ethical and moral issues are often left out of the conversation. Economics is a science, they tell us. It uses formulas; it measures and predicts, and moral issues cannot easily be figured into the equation. Maybe not, but we should consider that many of the most important things in this world are the things that do not yield easily to the scientific method.

Anyone experienced in managing complex systems knows they cannot function well without various dependable feedback loops. However, a major error of neoclassical economics is excluding social and environmental costs and over-relying on only one form of feedback: prices and markets. Unemployment and underemployment are feedback as well. Climate change is feedback. An economy seized up by fear—that's feedback, too.

Economists have taught us to reify the economy—that is, make it seem like a system of rules and regulations that are real and tangible, a system delivered from on high, a system that just *is*, like air or water, and is not amenable to change. But the system has been imagined by human beings, on assumptions made by human beings, and it can be changed by human beings.

Let us take a look at the values that run the country's economy—and our lives. We would have to use words such as *profit*, *production*, *efficiency*, *consumption*, and *creation of capital*. There is nothing wrong with these words, but they are not ends in themselves. They should exist to serve larger values, human values. They should serve the common good, human health and well-being, to ensure the care and sustainability of our earth.

The current economic meltdown will help us begin to ask the right questions. Does our economic system exist to serve families, or does our family structure exist to serve the economic structure? Why should both parents have to work out of the home? Are social structures arranged to bring generations together or pull them apart? Do work structures exist to support parenting, the building of community, and the work of citizen-activists, or for the efficiency of the economic machine?

Asking these questions is not a luxury but a necessity. When oil is no longer cheap—a time that will come again soon—our economic life will shift dramatically. We will be more locally focused. We will eat more local food, trade with small businesses close at hand, and find ways to work closer to home. We will often walk and bike and use mass transit instead of drive. Almost no one will fly thousands of miles away from home several times a year for meetings or vacations. We will live closer together, and we will share more of ourselves, more of the time. We will mend instead of buying new. Some of us urban dwellers will weave and knit and plant and grow. Change is already happening, and more will come.

The scales have fallen from our nation's eyes, and it is clear to almost everyone that the emperor has no clothes. The good news is that we will now have the opportunity to reimagine the kind of economy we want and the kind of life we want to live. People understand that we have a problem, but they have had their imaginations drained out of them by the constant barrage of messages they receive about consuming. They have had their energies drained by jobs that have longer and longer hours and less and less meaning. We need to take advantage of the moment, to reimagine, to re-form an American dream. Although we need leadership, leaders' sole authority is the people, and change always comes from the bottom up.

Those of us alive in these times have a clear and evident mission. We have a compelling moral purpose that can direct our lives and our energies: We are about saving the world. So what is our part? The place to begin is at home—that is, with ourselves. Notice what is life-denying and resist it. Live with the moral authority that comes from compassion and nonviolence. Form communities of people who will sustain you in living as you wish to live, whether they are study groups or alternative living arrangements or socially responsible, sustainable businesses. Our congregations must be central gathering places for such community.

You and I belong to a growing group of people—already over 25 percent of the U.S. population—that Paul Ray and Sherry Anderson refer to as the "cultural creatives," who value diversity, stewardship of the environment, economic justice, and civil rights for all. In their book, *Cultural Creatives*, Ray and Anderson say that roughly half this number combine these beliefs with some form of spiritual practice. They call these people the core cultural creatives. From these folks—folks like you and me, who populate Unitarian Universalist churches—the new story, the new cultural narrative, will emerge. I cannot know the exact words you will choose or how you will put them together for your story, but some of those words might be *love*, *service*, *kindness*, *joy*, *presence*, *peace*, *integrity*, *stewardship*, and *covenant*. These are religious concepts, and this is the beloved community that we are building.

I was intrigued by the words often attributed to East German dissident, Rudolf Behro: "When the forms of an old culture are dying, the new culture is created by a few people who are not afraid to be insecure." I started thinking about us as Unitarian Universalists. This is who we are—we are not afraid to be insecure. We are not afraid to search, to go deeper, to find the truth, even when the truth is unpalatable. We are seekers who want to live out of that truth, not some kind of made-up world that might be more comfortable to live in for the moment.

Unitarian Universalists, though few in number, can be the yeast in the loaf. However, let us be wary of the usual distractions and follies of our movement. It's grown-up time now. We no longer prioritize petty quarrels about how "religious" our language should be, conflicts between the humanists and the more spiritually inclined, or squabbles about who is in charge. The mission of the church is not to meet our needs; the mission of the church is to heal our world. It is to give ourselves to something larger than ourselves. Ironically, when we give of ourselves in this way, we find that our deepest needs are met.

The idealism that caused John Winthrop to say that we have a special destiny is not dead in this country. I see it in certain young people, who are quietly living in a way that respects our earth. I see it in creative people who have a vision far beyond the popular mind. I know that wherever the human spirit is willing to join with that larger spirit, new dreams can be dreamed and whole nations can be moved. Whoever thought the Berlin Wall would come crashing down? But when the time was right, down it came. Whoever thought that Nelson Mandela would get out of prison after 28 years and lead his nation? But, in time, it happened. I grew up in northern Louisiana in the 1950s in a small, totally segregated town; I never saw a black man in a dress shirt in my childhood or adolescence. Who would have guessed that I would see an African-American president in my lifetime? An African-American president, with a cabinet replete with women and people of color. The time is ripe for a great turning once again.

I am convinced that what is life-denying, what is repressive and false, will be known as such and that people, who are basically good, will follow a new way. Let us be some of those who step out and lead, who dare, once again, to bless the world.

We Are One

PETER MORALES

The hilly countryside of Chiapas is dotted everywhere with *milpas*, patches of corn. These milpas look nothing like the vast ocean of hybridized, fertilized, industrialized, subsidized corn that stretches from Nebraska to New York State. In Chiapas, the corn plants are farther apart, and the corn is mixed with beans and squash in an ancient, sustainable combination that produces a diet with all the essential amino acids. The corn is tended by hand, in little plots worked by individual families.

Chiapas is Mexico's southernmost state, bordering Guatemala. In both regions, impressive Mayan ruins dot the landscape and draw tourists. The descendants of that great civilization live today in abject poverty. The children are malnourished. Many cannot afford milk. Mayans are on the margins of society, living today, as they have for the past five hundred years, under an oppressive regime that denies their basic human rights.

My wife Phyllis and I traveled to Chiapas as part of a delegation sponsored by the Unitarian Universalist Service Committee. We met with people running nonprofit organizations, and we also met with Zapatista rebels struggling, with limited success, against centuries of oppression. They taught us about the intimate connections between the industrial corn of Iowa and the native corn in the milpas. Since the advent of the North American Free Trade Agreement (NAFTA), U.S. corn has been changing the Mexican economy. The corn tortilla, the staple of the Mexican diet, especially among the poor, is now typically made with U.S. corn. As demand for ethanol for U.S. gas guzzlers inflates the price of U.S. corn, the price of tortillas has skyrocketed. A little-known part of those NAFTA agreements required Mexico to change its laws that permitted *ejidos*, large areas of land owned communally for generations. The moneyed classes can now buy up land long owned by peasant families.

The richest man in the world is a Mexican, Carlos Slim. Slim is in fat city, worth more than Bill Gates or Warren Buffett, and getting richer at an amazing rate. He enjoys his wealth in a country where millions of children have insufficient food, a woeful education system, and no health care. It is an old story, little different from that of Europe or the United States. With rural families living on small plots of land being forced to leave, Chiapas is now a leading exporter of people. As thousands of economic refugees flee Chiapas, others from Central America cross Chiapas on their way north. They are heading for jobs at luxurious beach resorts filled with Americans and Europeans, or for the slums of Mexico City. Some of the most adventurous risk takers head for *la frontera*, the newly militarized border that tries to separate desperate Mexicanos from jobs in the United States. Hundreds die trying to cross the desert, and now there are Anglo vigilantes on the border attempting to "protect" America from the frightful prospect of more illegal immigrants. U.S. citizens are afraid, and their fear is stoked by reactionary ideologues and political opportunists in both major parties.

The illegal immigrants who are already here are afraid, too. There are about twelve million of them. They don't know when a raid by federal authorities will break up their families. Children don't know when their mother or father will be taken away. It happened not long ago in Greeley, Colorado. It is happening all over the country, and it is madness.

We live in a new America. My colleague Stan Perea calls it the America of the moo-shoo burrito and the Korean taco. California now has more people from minority populations than it has whites. Our country is now home to more Hispanics than African Americans. In most cities, the children entering the public schools speak more than seventy languages among them.

America was once defined by the movement of people who came to the east coast and moved westward. The new American story is of people moving north from countries to the south and moving to the west coast from countries in the Far East—such as Vietnam, Korea, and elsewhere.

In the case of the recent rapid increase in immigration from Mexico and Central America, most U.S. citizens tend to think we are somehow passive victims. These aliens are pouring over our border and must be stopped.

The truth is very different. Our economic policies, which disproportionately benefit the wealthy, are helping to create wrenching economic dislocations in Mexico, Guatemala, and Nicaragua. Many of the people trying to sneak into the United States were pushed out of their homes by U.S. policies.

I am not suggesting that our country does not need to control its borders, and I do not pretend to have all the policy answers. I do know this: We cannot pretend that we had nothing to do with the creation of this problem. I also know this: We are all connected. We are in this together.

Let us take a moment to get some historical perspective on our situation. Let us look at some major demographic events of the past five hundred years: The arrival of Europeans started a horrific pandemic in the Americas. It was worse than the plague in Europe and many times worse than AIDS. Native Americans had no resistance to the new diseases such as smallpox. Entire populations were wiped out. It was easy for Europeans to move west across North America because the Indian population had largely died off. The Native American population was a tiny fraction of what it had been in 1491.

Another major demographic move, of course, was the importation of African slaves. Slavery became the basis of an economy producing cotton and tobacco for an international market. The legacy of slavery, racism, and oppression still casts its shadow across America.

A hundred and seventy years ago, the slave-based economy with huge plantations growing commodities for export expanded westward across the South, but then it hit a border. What is now southeast Texas is prime land for growing cotton. The trouble was that it was part of Mexico. The border was porous, though, and undocumented Anglos poured across, bringing their slaves. They encountered another problem: Slavery was illegal in Mexico. The Anglo immigrants soon fomented a rebellion aimed at legalizing slavery. This is not radical left-wing revisionist history; this is the standard account of academic historians, and the version told on the University of Texas website. The fact that the white Texan revolt against Mexico was founded on the desire to extend black slavery has somehow never filtered down to what we teach in elementary schools. After winning their quick little war of independence, Texas joined the union as a slave state. Sadly, James Bowie, Davy Crockett, and Sam Houston were not the freedom-loving heroes we were once led to believe.

We need to see our present situation in its historical context. The border between the United States and Mexico was created to make space for slavery. We are building fences and guard towers along that border to keep Mexicans from reentering land that was taken from them. Of course, the Mexican elite, mostly of European descent, were not exactly blameless: The land that undocumented Americans stole from them was land they had previously stolen from Native Americans. It is easy to determine who has a *legal* right to be here, but who has a *moral* right to be here?

As a religious people who affirm human compassion, advocate for human rights, and seek justice, we must never make the mistake of confusing a legal right with a moral right. The forced removal of Native Americans from their land and onto reservations was legal. The importation and sale of African slaves was legal. South African apartheid was legal. The confiscation of the property of

Jews at the beginning of the Nazi regime was legal. The Spanish Inquisition was legal. Crucifying Jesus was legal. Burning Michael Servetus at the stake for his unitarian theology was legal. The fact that something is legal does not cut much ethical ice. The powerful have always used the legal system to oppress the powerless.

It is true that as citizens we should respect the rule of law. More importantly, though, our duty is to create laws founded on our highest sense of justice, equity, and compassion. Loud voices urge us to choose fear, denial, reactionary nationalism, and racism. We must resist and choose the better way urged by every major religious tradition. We must choose the path of compassion and hope. We must choose a path that is founded on the recognition that we are connected, that we are all in this together.

These are the teachings of every great tradition. At the core of the teachings of Jesus is the conviction that we are all one. We are all God's children, and we are all equal. We are supposed to care for one another. Jesus taught his followers that an act of kindness to the most humble human being was the equivalent of performing the same for Jesus.

The prophet Muhammad taught that the tribal divisions among the Arabian people were wrong. The symbols of those tribal divisions were the legion of tribal gods, and Muhammad told the people that these gods were false, that there is only one God. We are united, and we owe our allegiance to the one creator.

Buddhism teaches that if we stop and really pay attention, we will realize that the things we think separate us are an illusion. Our connections are ultimately real, not our divisions.

We find the same message in every tradition: We are one. We are connected. We are brothers and sisters. If we truly accept that we are all part of a greater whole, that what unites and transcends us is ultimately more important than our illusion of individuality, how might that guide us? If we accept that compassion (literally "to suffer with") is the manifestation of realizing that we are one, what are the implications? What would our community and our state and our nation do if they were guided by the finest aspirations of humanity's religions? What would you and I do if we were guided by these very same ideas, as expressed in our Unitarian Universalist Principles? What future might we build if we created policies guided by our notions of justice, equity, and compassion in human relations?

I do not have all the policy answers on immigration or the related issues of public education, health care, and the economy. I do know this: Breaking up poor working families who have lived among us for years does not feel like justice, equity, and compassion in action. Refusing minimal health services to young children does not feel like the way we should treat members of our human family. Having our police forces profile brown people does not feel like breaking down the walls of tribalism. Creating a huge wall, complete with barbed wire, across hundreds of miles of border does not feel neighborly.

There must be a better way, and you and I must help build it. Barbed wire is not the answer. More border guards and more deportations are not the answer. Paranoia and panic will solve nothing.

We must remember that we are all immigrant stock, every single one of us living on this continent. Even Native Americans at one time immigrated here from Asia.

We must also acknowledge that we helped to create the situation in which displaced people look to find a home here. America has already been transformed by the latest waves of immigration. Our children and grandchildren are going to live in a multicultural society—a society of moo-shoo burritos, egg roll tacos, and whole wheat tortillas. We need not be afraid of that multicultural society. Fear leads to violence and repression.

Instead, let us embrace the possibilities before us. Let us be guided by love and hope. Let our actions emerge from the deep conviction that people from Mexico and Korea and Canada and Vietnam are ultimately part of our extended family. Surely, religious people who have learned to embrace the wisdom of Judaism, Christianity, humanism, Islam, and Eastern religions can lead the way. We are people who have always affirmed human diversity.

We have always looked to the future and seen new possibilities. We must do so again. Let us be the people who break down the arbitrary barriers that divide us from them. We are one, and love and hope will guide us. Let us, together with all our brothers and sisters, build a new way.

The Sacraments of the Word and Celebration

VICTORIA SAFFORD

How does our faith hold brokenness, injustice, and suffering?

Clumsily. Gingerly. Tenderly. Bravely. Lovingly. Reverently. Humbly and deliberately. Imperfectly.

One by one, we hold brokenness in our blood and bones and memory as human beings susceptible to hurt and betrayal, mercy and grace. We respond every day in ways that are bold and ways that are skittish or selfish, ways radiantly healthy and ways tragic, dangerous, and flawed. As Unitarian Universalists, we hold brokenness collectively, communally, theologically—in covenant with each other in congregations and with the circles of community that bind us by circumstance and choice. Yet the work of holding brokenness begins within each of us singly, deeply, privately, perhaps not even consciously, whenever we re-member the fragments of our story, whenever our imagination expands to acknowledge and embrace the plain and radiant humanity of someone else. In congregations, this expansion of the heart (and mind and soul) is our principal work. Our most urgent question as individuals and in communities is thus, How can we hold brokenness, injustice, and suffering, with wide open eyes and open arms, and at the same time greet the day with gladness, with gratitude and hope, with forgiveness, with love of life and of one another? We can begin with the sacrament of the living word and the sacrament of celebration.

On Sunday mornings especially but also other times, we tell sacred stories. They come from scripture and the *New York Times*; they come from poems and other art, newly made or handed down through generations; they come from people's living memory, people we know or somehow know about. Martin Espada calls it *el coro*, the chorus of voices singing humanity's song of the soul, sometimes joyful and triumphant, but also and especially the sorrow songs of oppression, repression, injustice, poverty, prejudice, and the consequences of empire—all the beautiful, terrible stories and songs.

The church exists, in part, to remember—to rescue from a vast silence the stories that might not otherwise be heard, to ask questions that might not elsewhere be asked, to celebrate victories and mourn losses that might otherwise be forgotten, to bless what might go unblessed. This remembering, this naming of truth, the consecration of stories forgotten, forbidden, and hidden, both terrible and beautiful, is the sacrament of the living word.

Here is one such story from near the place where I live. Near the corner of Second Avenue East and First Street in Duluth, Minnesota, stands a statue of three young men, college-aged, strong and hopeful, looking out of the stone onto the world. On a summer night in 1920, these three—Isaac McGhie, Elias Clayton, and Elmer Jackson—were lynched on that spot by a mob that may have numbered as many as ten thousand people. The three were road workers for a traveling circus, arrested days before on charges of raping a white woman. The crowd broke into the jail and dragged them to a lamppost. It did not take very long for these thousands of citizens to gather themselves around a murderous idea. Not even the circus would have brought out ten thousand people without notice.

Evil was easily organized, as it so often is, from the fragments of possibility that lie around ever ready, the tiny sharp shards of potential, the fertile seeds that exist inside each one of us. Of the ten thousand, a few were masterminds but most were "merely" spectators, carrying no weapons, no premeditated coils of rope.

However, it is not always easy to draw those lines. So often evil shows itself not as a monolith but as a delicate mosaic composed of a great many very small pieces. Each person present in the crowd had been prepared for what he or she did that night, by songs and stories and by the echoing silence of stories untold.

In 2003, a different crowd gathered in that street, some of them descendants of those who had been present the first time. The people of Duluth—African Americans and white Americans and others—came together to tell this story out loud, publicly, to claim shared ownership of their history (our history) hidden for decades like a festering family secret. The monument they dedicated displays the words of Edmund Burke: "An event has happened upon which it is difficult to speak and impossible to remain silent."

Unitarian Universalism often stands accused of remaining silent, of being "soft on crime," unwilling to look evil in the eye and admit that some human beings, by their choices, have stepped across an invisible but absolute line, forfeiting forgiveness. The early Universalists did believe that every person is redeemable, salvageable, possessed of worth and even dignity no matter what, but this was less a statement about human nature than about the nature of God, who was, for them, love and nothing else, understanding and nothing less—forgiveness absolutely, if one would be forgiven. The real concern of the Universalists, and an abiding concern for their descendants, was judgment: who gets to do it, and on what grounds. Who is fit to say whose soul might be beyond repair? They disbelieved, vehemently, in the eternal punishment of hell, but not in hell entirely. They held that we are punished not for our sins but *by* them, every day; that in the soul something shrivels, disintegrates, and starts to die when we collaborate with evil. Our wholeness, our holiness, is torn; our spirit becomes sick. They disbelieved in the doctrine of original sin, at least as it was roared from raging pulpits, but more, they disbelieved in the myth of original goodness: that there ever was a golden age, an innocent time when happy human beings tended the garden of the earth and then made some kind of awful first mistake. There was no mistake, they said, no apple and no snake. Free will was inherent in us all along. We make hell for one another while we live, they said, by cruel action and selfish inaction; sometimes we make hell for ourselves, and live there, sort of, till we die.

Evil is the capacity within us and among us to break the sacred connection with ourselves, with each other, with the holy, and further, to deny this breakage or to call it virtue. The soil in which evil flourishes is a rich compost of ignorance, arrogance, fear, and delusion, mostly self-delusion. Sunlight beats it back. Humility stunts its growth. Truth telling, truth seeking, truth speaking, secret-breaking, brave naming, bearing witness—these things weaken its resolve. It is good practice to teach children and carve into stone the words, "Here happened an event upon which it is difficult to speak and impossible to remain silent." This is how sacred connection begins and how it is restored. This is part of what the church is for.

Some months ago, I read an article in the *New York Times* about bookstores in Baghdad, old shops that once were bright cultural centers where writers, artists, philosophers, and passersby gathered to talk politics and literature. One bookseller says that now people rarely linger to talk, certainly never about politics, and they do not buy poetry or history. All he can sell are religious tracts and manuals for cell phones, the stuff of fear and practical survival. One woman recalls that even under Saddam Hussein, when books were banned and writers imprisoned, people still met in secret to talk about culture and art. But not now. She remembers attending secret meetings to read illegal photocopies of classical Iraqi literature, saying, "To us, it was like oxygen." When Saddam's regime was toppled, some believed that life might yet return to what it once had been. Her husband began a diary, interviewing neighbors and relatives, writing down their hopes and dreams. It seems silly now, she says—so many of their friends have been killed and no one goes outside. One man who loved the old bookstores worries about what happens to a country in which the young people have no cultural or intellectual memory, no spiritual imagination, no interest in it; what happens when they're reading only computer manuals and fundamentalist brochures. "They can read, they can write, but they can't understand. That's good for dictatorship and dangerous for democracy. It's a spare army for all hard-line elements."

An ordinary man who records in his journal the ordinary, extraordinary memories and dreams of his people exemplifies the role of the prophetic church. In this postinaugural moment, in every moment, the liberal church exists to be a keeper of sacred stories. We should be out there right now, asking everyone not who they voted for, but what they voted for and why, asking, like that man in Baghdad, "What are your hopes for our country now, for our world? What are your best memories of what it might become? What are your clear dreams of what it must not become again?"

History is recorded memory, multifaceted, multilayered, multilingual, always incomplete, and sung in a chorus of voices often at odds with each other and always, by necessity, biased. History is the record not of what happened but of what is recalled, what will be brought forward and redeemed. Religion holds the accumulated memories and hopes of community, rendered mythically, in stories the people cherish, change, and pass on. In these stories, the people's mistakes are told, their losses laid out, and their dreams of reconciliation and redemption given form. In these stories, people map out the promised land, that place that must always, it turns out, be of their own making. They keep remembering out loud not only where they've been but where they mean to go, what manner of people they would be, and what manner of people they are.

When Russian poet Anna Akhmatova's life was threatened, she devised a way to continue bearing witness to the horrors of Stalin's regime: Whenever she wrote a new poem, she invited a friend over to memorize it, and then she burned the only copy. Her friends carried in their bodies the body of her work, and that living library survived. I think of a slender volume called *Poems from Guantanamo*, published in 2007 and written by detainees from many countries, mostly in Arabic. These, too, were memorized, whispered defiantly and deliberately from one man's mouth to another man's ear, and on and on through all the corridors and buildings. Some were etched on Styrofoam cups, which were passed quietly from cell to cell, then cradled gently in the bottom of a trash bag and saved by a guard or kitchen worker, complicit guardians of holy scripture.

This is what I have come to believe about human beings: We require food, water, shelter, air, and stories. Something in us needs to speak and to be heard, to forgive and be forgiven, to sing and hear music, to speak our truth and listen for the truths of others. Because we are human beings—religious human beings, bound to one another and to sacred mystery—part of our calling is to aid and abet the transmission of beauty and truth.

What readings, from what voices, will you choose for Sunday morning? What music will you have the people sing? In what long arc of sacred human history will you set the little agenda of the Social Action Committee? Whose portraits will hang on the walls of the classrooms to teach children and remind their parents of holiness and grace? What holy days shall we observe? All these things hold suffering, brokenness, evil, and injustice, by what I have called the sacrament of the word, or the sacrament of story. There exists also the sacrament of celebration, for which the church is also responsible. Marge Piercy has a poem called "The Art of Blessing the Day," in which she calls out a litany of ordinary miracles: sun after rain, rain after drought, lost cats found and lost love restored, ripe peaches and big summer tomatoes. She then speaks of political victory, and the dancing, the gladness, the wild joy we are called to when promised change becomes, for a moment, palpable and real. This, she says, "is the blessing for the rising of the bread, the sun, the oppressed." This is in part what worship is for, this thankfulness, this wonder and rejoicing, this other way of intimate connection with those who have gone before and those who may be dancing even now, whose names we cannot know but whose love of life we share.

Paul Lakeland, in *Postmodernity*, writes about language and creativity, "What can be said lays down the boundary of what can be thought." Because we mean to give serious thought in our congregations not only to brokenness and sorrow but also to wholeness and healing, to restoration and hope and beloved community, we paint those bright pictures also. We sing the glad songs as loudly and bravely as we can, partly so that we can imagine the future and partly because, like some other communions, we hold despair to be a sin.

On those occasions when the weight of the world is closing in and the evidence against hope mounts as I read the news, when I start confusing cynicism with pragmatism and begin muttering miserable, unrepeatable things at the radio, when I sigh, "I'm so tired. I'm so discouraged"—at those times, my partner, Ross, will say, in the kindest possible way, "What kind of self-indulgent whining is this? What kind of entitled grandiosity of privilege is this, to think that you or I or anyone has the right to sever the bright thread of hope, the tradition of dedication to the common good and faith in people's power to imagine great change, to imagine and take great risks? There is a beautiful, proud history of work for human rights and freedom, for social change and peace and protection of the earth. This is the story in which we choose to stand. This is not the story of oppression and imperialism and militarism and corporate greed and plunder, but that alternative story, equally true, of those who lived their lives and gave their lives for love, for a difficult and truly patriotic ideal—liberty and justice for all. This is an ideal that is gradually gathering up everyone—women and slaves and indigenous people; children and elders and the poor and the sick; the mentally ill; the workers, the farmers, the immigrants; those fighting for human rights and civil rights, for public schools and pluralism; every person, gay and straight, who would sit at the welcome table. We're only here to pass this story on," Ross tells me. "All you have to do is keep the fire burning for a little while, stoke it with your life, don't allow it to go out, and pass it on. You have no right to put it out." Not in so many words—but that's about what Ross will say.

This is what we say every Sunday. The sacrament of celebration involves memory as much as it involves forward-looking hope. The church can hold evil and injustice only if it also holds the story of resistance. It is not the mourning alone but the singing that will move our people out of the sanctuary and into the street, into the statehouse, where the life of prayer is embodied, compassion becomes commitment, and love lives and breathes as justice.

Our Story

WILLIAM SINKFORD

In spring of 2009, I spent a few days in Alabama with the Vision Legacy Tour, a pilgrimage to Selma, Montgomery, and other key sites in the civil rights struggle of the 1960s. The Unitarian Universalist presence in these places in those times offers a compelling story, one we are proud to tell:

> Selma, 1965. Black protestors demanding the right to vote try to march to the state capital via the Pettus Bridge, where they are met by fire hoses and beaten back. The day becomes known as Bloody Sunday. Dr. Martin Luther King, Jr., calls for white clergy to come stand with him and the local black community; the Unitarian Universalist Association Board answers the call and travels as a group from Boston to Selma, where dozens more Unitarian Universalist ministers join them. Rev. James Reeb is killed by a group of angry whites as he and two colleagues leave a diner in town, becoming a UU martyr. Dr. King gives the eulogy for Reeb at Brown Chapel. President Lyndon Johnson, moved to action by the scenes of violence broadcast over network television from Selma, sends federal troops. With their protection, the marchers cross the Pettus Bridge and proceed to Montgomery. Photographs show Rev. Dana Greeley, first president of the UUA, march-

ing in the rank directly behind Dr. King and Rev. Ralph Abernathy. Viola Liuzzo, a UU laywoman from Detroit, is killed outside Selma while transporting black protestors, becoming the second known UU martyr in the civil rights movement. Within the year, Johnson signs the Voting Rights Act into law.

UUs have chosen these events as a foundational story about our faith and its engagement with race. It is a success story. It makes us feel good. The issue was clear, and our faith answered the call. Two of our number gave their lives in the cause of justice. We were just, we were brave, and we were innocent; no wonder we retell this story to our children and to ourselves. A memorial to the Selma martyrs (including a young black man, Jimmy Lee Jackson, who was the first killed in this particular chapter of the civil rights story) graces the chapel at our home office at 25 Beacon Street in Boston. I organized its dedication in my first year as president.

We are happy to claim many other stories with similar characteristics. In the 1850s, Theodore Parker preached from the Federal Street Church pulpit with a loaded gun by his side, lest officials try to arrest the fugitive slaves in the sanctuary. In the 1950s, the First Unitarian Church of Chicago bought newspaper ads inviting people of color to visit and join the congregation, and they did. The Racial and Cultural Diversity resolution passed unanimously at the 1992 Calgary General Assembly. Perhaps even the 2001 vote that elected me the first African American to head a predominantly white denomination may fall in this category of stories we are happy to tell.

These are stories of courage, of success, of moral clarity, of leadership on the cutting edge of the cause of justice. They make us feel good about ourselves.

The difficulty is not claiming these stories as part of our history, our identity, our definition of who we are as a religious people. Since the stories are true, we should know them and even allow ourselves to be proud. The difficulty is that there are so many other stories about our faith's engagement with race that we do not claim. Unitarians were involved with and profited from the transatlantic slave trade. There was widespread Unitarian and Universalist opposition to the abolition of slavery. The UU Church of Atlanta, Georgia, refused to admit black members in the 1950s, ultimately leading the American Unitarian Association to close the church. Beginning in the 1950s, UUs fled the cities to segregated suburbs, resulting in the closing of many center city churches. In the late 1980s and 1990s, there was a failed attempt to launch new biracial congregations. (Only one of these survives as an autonomous faith community. I had the painful task of closing most of them when I joined the UUA staff in 1994.) Key leadership groups resisted the inclusion of antiracism as an important mission-based priority in the 1990s, as the Journey toward Wholeness program was developed. Ministers of color have been rejected, and some still have trouble finding successful parish settlements. All too frequently, candidates of color are rejected during the ministerial search process in our congregations, and the ministers of color have faced difficulties in building successful parish settlements.

Of all the stories we have incorporated into our identity as a people, perhaps the most important is the black empowerment controversy that began in 1968. Anyone retelling a story of this complexity should feel considerable trepidation, confident only that any account will displease some, perhaps all. These are the bare bones as I know them:

> Following the assassination of Martin Luther King, Jr., in 1968 (just three years after the events in Selma), black communities in American cities erupt in violence; national broadcasters bring the riots into the nation's living rooms. At a conference convened by the UUA to imagine a response to this violence, a caucus of black UUs forms and makes demands of the Association.
>
> The 1968 UUA General Assembly passes the caucus's demand for $1,000,000 in reparations for black economic

> development, to be administered by black UUs. The tumultuous process leading up to the vote includes a walkout by many black UUs, white allies, and youth. Not all blacks join the walkout. In response, an integrated group (Black and White Action) forms and demands funding. Congregations and families, including my own, are torn between the separatist and integrationist approaches.
>
> In 1969, new UUA president Bob West faces a financial crisis as a result of Greeley administration policies, and just over half of the promised $1,000,000 is ever paid. Many black UUs, including me, leave the faith feeling deeply betrayed. Unitarian Universalism, in most material respects, withdraws from engagement with racial justice. It was just too hard. Coincidentally or not, these events ushered in a steady decline in reported congregational membership that lasted until the mid-1980s.

Feelings ran very high throughout the black empowerment controversy. Dana Greeley pushed his way to the front of the line at a microphone so that he could speak against the reparations. People spat at one another. This was not who we thought we were. People on both sides of the controversy were so embittered that some individuals on both sides refused to enter the UUA's administrative offices at 25 Beacon Street until I became president in 2001.

You can see why we dislike this story. It is a story of conflict and failure, not success. We saw one another as enemies. The question of who stood on the side of justice was a matter of genuine disagreement, and innocence could be claimed by no one. This story does not make us feel good, and we do not want to revisit it.

I am not arguing that we should simply replace the Selma story, that story of triumph at the heart of our identity around race, with the black empowerment story, that story of conflict and failure. I do believe that we have to be able to claim both as part of our heritage, for there are reasons neither story is adequate on its own, or even when paired with the other.

First, both of these stories suggest that race is an issue concerning blacks and whites. They render invisible the Native American, Asian, and Latino communities that have been a part of "we the people" all along. We need a story that will allow us to move into a multicultural future in which racial and cultural identity is often complex.

Second, these are stories from over forty years ago. As evidenced in essays in this volume by Adam Gerhardstein and Kat Liu, younger UUs in the millennial generation have grown up with racial diversity. Life in a multicultural community is normative for them, and the stories of our triumphs in relationships between blacks and whites have little relevance.

Third, and most importantly, these stories provide insufficient spiritual grounding for the challenges and opportunities that UUs face in the twenty-first century. Today, issues of immigration and immigrant rights have to be on our screen. Today, thanks to transracial adoption and blended families, most of our church schools are significantly multicultural even if our pews are not. Today, the numbers of adults of color in our congregations have perceptibly increased. Today, forty ministers of color serve our congregations, more serve in community ministries, and more than forty seminarians of color prepare for our ministry. Once these students are ordained and begin serving our congregations, ministers of color will constitute 10 percent of active UU parish ministers.

Some of our congregations have embraced this multicultural future. The blending of the All Souls Tulsa Church (mostly white) with the New Dimensions congregation (mostly black) is a recent case in point. We need to make room in our story not just for past successes and failures but for the challenges of our current context. Making room will require changing some of our language of self-identity. To describe Unitarian Universalism as a predominantly white faith is accurate but not helpful. The phrase contains not one iota of our aspirations, and it locks us in a spirit-deadening acceptance of demographic determinism.

What is our story about Unitarian Universalism and race? And what story do we need? On a pilgrimage to Africa in November

2008, I learned several lessons from the South African Truth and Reconciliation process. The South African people's commitment to discovering and telling the truth allowed them to move beyond apartheid without swinging into the chaos of retribution. Similarly, UUs must own and tell both sides of our history—the triumphs and the failures—but this only sets the stage for the real work. As Mary Burton, one of the original Truth and Reconciliation commissioners, said to me, "I have to work at reconciliation every day of my life."

The religious voice was critical in South Africa. I felt privileged to meet leaders such as Archbishop Desmond Tutu, who time and time again stood in the center of controversy and said, "We are one people and we can be reconciled." Several people I met said Tutu had been a broken record on this point, and his vision of the beloved community finally prevailed.

UUs need to claim a story of struggle, an unabashedly religious story that can name our successes and our failures, our courage and our cowardice, our sacrifice and our privilege. That story will be aspirational, for at times we have retreated from the call of justice, yet over the long haul, we have always reengaged. Our story of struggle is grounded in our faith, values, and tradition, taking the inherent worth and dignity of every person and the fundamental reality of our interconnectedness not as idle phrases but as calls to action. This story of struggle will not only put our history in perspective but empower us to face the challenges of the days ahead.

The two current UU stories about race have left us divided. Some of us, probably most, choose the Selma narrative of success, but we know in our hearts that our work is far from done. Others choose the black empowerment narrative and find it hard to honor the courage that is legitimately a part of our history. Even worse, among those in my generation, feelings are still so strong that even discussing our history feels dangerous. We need a story that can bring us together. The story we tell about ourselves as a people is our choice. May we choose well.

Stories from the Future

JILL SCHWENDEMAN

Her hands are folded around her knee. Though her sunhat suggests she could be at a picnic, her grandmotherly face wears an expression of defiance. Peeking at her from our position behind the policemen, we see that in her calm, she is a wall. The officers' guns and billy clubs are holstered, but the men tower over her, a menacing frame.

This is a photograph of Dorothy Day at a United Farm Workers protest in 1973. The picture sat in the front room of my in-laws' house. It fascinated my twin sons, who gazed at it long and hard when they were just toddlers. It captured something powerful, although the boys were not certain exactly what that was. When we visited, they never failed to find the photo and pepper us with questions: Who is this woman? What is happening here? Each time, I had to correct one son on a fact he kept misremembering. No, I'd tell him, this was not a photo of Grandma's sister.

It was not surprising that he should expect she was a relative. He comes from a line of rabble-rousers, including graceful women who made agitating their life's mission. Their grandmother represents people on death row. She wrote, "When I was little, the nuns at my school showed us pictures of children living on the streets of Rio de Janeiro. Those pictures are branded on my brain. They enlivened something in me that has never gone away. I am who I am because of those pictures. I'm sure it is why I do what I do."

Last year, I was informed by members of my congregation's youth group that Archbishop Desmond Tutu is very short. He gives good hugs, they told me, and he is prone to an infectious giggle. The teens were our delegates to a conference of PeaceJam, a leadership development organization that seeks to inspire and equip young people for lives of purpose. Through PeaceJam, youth have been introduced to eleven Nobel laureates. The curriculum is excellent, but the most important learning happens around the edges, when the teens share an elevator with an icon like Tutu or give him a hug. Our young people saw that Archbishop Tutu, world-renowned advocate for justice, is also just one of us—a flesh-and-blood person who brushes his teeth in the morning, puts on his pants just like anyone else, and enjoys a good laugh. Like a cherished relative, he has become part of their frame of reference.

A few years ago, members of our congregation and our minister lent a hand with a class we called Voices of Resistance. They affirmed the youth group's record of soul-searching and social action. They read teens stories about people of conscience, history laced with humor and courage. They traced our Unitarian Universalist lineage, including abolitionists, environmentalists, peace organizers, activists against racism, reformers who stood for freedom of conscience, and others—up to and including the quiet giants in our own congregation.

There is a tension inherent in Unitarian Universalism: What does it mean to make a tradition of rabble rousing? We study our remarkable, imperfect history while embracing the ongoing search for meaning and truth. Ours is a free faith, characterized not by the recitation of a creed but by principles that guide, without defining, its expression in each age.

Being young may help position people for prophetic leadership. Gandhi first organized others to fight ethnic prejudice at the age of twenty-four. The worried parents of twelve-year-old Jesus found him on the steps of the temple, conversing with religious leaders in awe of his erudition. Martin Luther King, Jr., was twenty-six when he led the Montgomery bus boycott and mobilized students across the south. Months before police arrested Rosa Parks, fifteen-year-old Claudette Clovin was led off a bus in handcuffs and thrown into an Alabama jail.

UU adolescents are living their own new stories. For example, the youth of our congregation brought the United Nation's antipoverty Millennium Goals into worship services and the coffee hour, mobilizing the congregation to send twelve hundred handwritten advocacy letters. Our PeaceJam group studied the life of a Nobel Peace Prize winner, promoted fair trade locally, made microloans to impoverished entrepreneurs abroad, and folded peace cranes to send to a UU congregation struck by violence. Similar youth activism is in evidence throughout the Association.

Stories of vision and action, whether they come from children, youth, or adults, invigorate our evolving faith. Youth ministry is not just for youth, by youth, or even with youth. It is ministry by and for the entire congregation. It is the work of our faith.

A teen in our youth group had long tussled with questions of faith when she was invited to present a "This I Believe" statement to the congregation. She did a beautiful job and people rushed to compliment her afterward. However, when I asked her what the experience had been like, she hesitated. She was glad people had found her articulate and poised, she said, but mostly she wanted to know what everyone had thought of her ideas. What did they have to add or critique? More than an object of amazed pride, she wanted to be a partner in dialogue.

I know a grown woman who also thought she perceived surprise in over-strenuous compliments. Behind an all-white audience's messages that she was a good speaker, she heard, "for a Puerto Rican." The tacit qualifiers alienated her. Intentionally or not, it is easy to discount people unlike ourselves. Consider the well-meaning adult who, upon seeing a child's beautiful painting, exclaims, "You'll be an artist *some day*."

A few years down the road, the teen speaker's arguments will likely be more informed and nuanced. Her value for young people, though, may be weaker when she is no longer their peer, and the voice she can offer all of us from the perch of her adolescence will be eclipsed by the perspective of an older self. The child painter, too, will likely grow in technique, but he will leave behind something unique and irreplaceable. If we are focused on what we imagine he can accomplish in the future, we might miss the present contributions of a child who is already an artist in his own right.

Jesus taught that important lessons sometimes come from surprising sources. Feminist theologian Susan Thistlethwaithe described how she was stretched when her child pointed out the unfairness of a book title, *Men of God*. Thistlethwaithe proudly praised the little one for seeing that the title excluded women. Exasperated, her child replied, "*No,* it should say 'men, women, and *children* of God!'" Congregations are places where we practice living our ideals. They are places where we can also make mistakes, as Thistlethwaithe did, and work to correct them. We know from science that failures can be as valuable as successes, suggesting as they do a better way to proceed. Children and youth, exemplars at learning through "play and do" investigation, may in this sense be more UU than their elders!

Except for the span from birth to age three, there is no period of human development as profound as adolescence in terms of physical, psychological, spiritual, and social change. Youth minister Kenda Creasy Dean wrote in her essay "Fessing Up: Owning Our Theological Commitments" that teens are "theologians by nature, uniquely wired for theological reflection because questions about who we are in relationship to 'the gods' form the spine of the human search for the self. . . . Children can't cognitively think in the perspective of another, but adolescents can—an extraordinary mental achievement that literally changes their position in the world." Teens ask questions that are religious in nature: Who am I? Why am I here? Who am I in relation to others? As they forge a new self-identity, they question authority, seek greater freedom, self-determination, and develop passion for righting wrongs. The active quest, the open eyes, the heart yearning for things to be set right—these are not only teen traits but are goals of Unitarian

Universalism. They are spiritual gifts that young people bring to our faith.

Adolescents, who are neither children nor adults, show unevenness in the skill sets needed to function successfully as adults—planning ahead, communicating frustration without aggression, and negotiating complex social situations, for instance. However, their increasing impulse control adds power to their decision-making ability, as they learn to weigh options for action against their higher values. Rather than abandoning teens during this critical developmental stage, it is crucial that congregations provide encouragement, companionship, and guidance.

The most effective teaching is nested within a relational framework. Psychologist Lev Vygotsky identified what he called the *zone of proximal development*—the range of activities between what a learner can do independently and with assistance. Vygotsky taught that a teacher's role is to help the learners stretch outward the growing edge of their abilities. Think of the toddler who thrusts her sippy cup toward her father and declares, "Cub!" Intuitively using a process called scaffolding, Dad says, "Yes, honey! That's a cup! That's a *blue* cup." Looking quizzically at the cup in her hand, the child repeats, "Boo cub." The engine of learning is not just her own bold effort, but her relationship with a parent who understands her. A multigenerational religious community recognizes that each person, as well as the congregation as a whole, has a zone of proximal development. As teens and others stretch into new powers of relational skill, so can the congregation itself gain new capacities and powers of choice. Congregations thrive by creating safe environments of mutual accountability, then setting high aspirations, and celebrating attempts to reach toward the goals, whether the attempts succeed or fail.

In the congregation I serve, we adults tenderly plant a simple message in our children: "This is the church of the open mind, the loving heart, and the helping hands. Together we care for our earth and work for friendship and peace in our world." We add a sprinkle of good deeds and the light of kindness. We pray that each child's spirit will grow skyward, a sturdy tree, a place for nesting and respite. We fend off whatever nibbles at it. We pour on it our love and our hopes. We worry over the ground, wishing the soil could be richer and provide some perfect food for this miracle.

Mostly what we do, though, is make space, and hope. The tree has its own life. It seeks the sun insistently. We watch in wonder as it offers fruit and breath, a home. Then, some searing day, we find our shoulder cooled by new shade. The tree is both a blessing from our past and a prayer from the unfolding future.

We know that young people can bring a vibrant faith to bear on the future because we understand the past that created the fertile ground of today. Rosa Parks refused to give up her seat on the bus not only because she was tired but also because she had been studying nonviolence with other activists. The Student Non-Violence Coordinating Committee patterned its strategy on Gandhi's example. Gandhi did not create his techniques out of whole cloth but applied his interpretations to ancient Indian traditions. By recognizing the sources that fed heroes such as these, we locate our own lives on a storyline with a long past and a promising future.

Unitarian Universalism asks us to be faithful not only to ourselves but also to the society in which we are embedded. From the moment of our conception, none of us exists except in relation to others. At its best, youth ministry models this radical mutuality through the spiritual discipline of open-hearted engagement with one another. This mutuality involves a commitment to receive and be received by one another in a formative way. Right relationship prevails when we nurture vibrant interpersonal webs and welcome the gifts, joys, and burdens of all, receiving and being received. The discipline of mutuality builds congregations responsive to the particulars of our place and time.

When congregants receive one another in both love and challenge, they inhabit the covenant implicit in our principles. Staying in covenant requires courage, respect, forgiveness, and a sense of humor. It means wrestling with inevitable shock points, such as a teen's loud music, the young person who acts like an adult one moment and a child the next, or the surprisingly articulate young speaker. A congregation that does this work becomes what Linda LaPlante calls a "laboratory of human interaction." Here, people of faith hone new skills and try again when things are not going well, even when it would be easier to walk away in disgust or bafflement.

When a congregation's driving force is mutuality, teaching is not just something adults do. Instead, information, stories, imagination, and inspiration swirl dynamically between generations. Within this microcosm of the beloved community, differences have generative potential. Every individual, from the shining-eyed baby to the sullen teen to the person who has just lost a job, contributes uniquely to the ongoing formation of our collective identity. When we listen for the unamplified voices, we learn a habit of watching for other kinds of exclusion as well. Where questions are welcomed, those who felt on the outside find a home. Mutuality blesses the messy, ongoing pursuit of right relationship and beloved community, and their manifestation in the here and now.

Around the time my youngest child turned five, he was fascinated with the concept that kids keep getting physically larger until they are grown-ups. "Mommy," he said once, "I'm bigger than you, because I am still growing." Truer words were never spoken! He and I are bound together by love and commitment, which make us pliable and confident. I have power to influence him, but he also has power to influence me. When people experience commitment and respect, they feel free to take risks, learn, and grow. Likewise, congregations that embrace an all-church model of ministry create a culture of mutuality and experimentation. They become sacred places for comfort and challenge, acceptance and growth, security and openness. They embody our tradition of responding to the particular struggles of each age, and as such, they are engines for this faith. They live at the growing edge of Unitarian Universalism.

Educating for Social Change

MARK A. HICKS

Living in Washington DC provides ample opportunities to learn about the rhythm of life surrounding the Chesapeake Bay. I often marvel at the dramatic moltings a female blue crab endures, shedding her old shell to grow a new, larger one. During this seventy-two-hour stage of transformation, her skin is tissue-soft, translucent, permeable—no protection from the predators (including those of us who find soft-shell crab a delicacy!) who hunt the grasses and shallows of the bay, sensing the crab's presence, seeking to cut off the possibility of her future. An average blue crab molts twenty-seven times over the course of a lifetime. Remaining alive requires navigating the world when most vulnerable—year after year—in order to emerge hardened, larger, and ready to face down bigger challenges.

The molting blue crab is an instructive metaphor for teaching for social change. Over time, educators have learned much about how unyielding structures, emotional contradictions, and cognitive and emotional dissonance impede the journey toward justice. Year after year, we too must find ways to do justice in environments where we must be suspicious of oppressive systems that seek to use us for their own purposes. Thus, the educator's job is to provide pedagogical structures that help learners stand firm against oppressive constructs while remaining vulnerable enough to develop more expansive, inclusionary habits of mind and practice. What kind of environment is supportive enough to let people shed old practices and bad habits of mind in favor of more inclusive frames of reference? What skills can educators teach that help justice workers develop the delicate artistry involved in shifting paradigms? How do we create learning experiences that promote growth and connection to the worldviews most compatible with Unitarian Universalist faith? And after all that contextualizing and skill building, how do we help ourselves and our colleagues sustain a culture that fosters growth in a climate fraught with danger?

Helping individuals and groups experience paradigmatic shifts requires engaging with them in a process that goes beyond logic. Both empirical research and practices of teaching and learning show that a symbiotic relationship forms when hope is coupled with action. Going against the grain when following our principles can bring a victorious sense of hope, enhancing the likelihood and frequency of future action. We have seen this cycle manifest itself throughout history and in our own lives. Teenagers, hopeful that desegregation would end, took action by sitting at lunch counters, leading others to believe they could bring about similar results. Physical trainers say that the more success people have with producing physical results, the more likely it is that they will stick with the regime. Writing coaches urge students to write every day, even if only briefly, knowing such discipline reinforces one's identity as a writer, especially when self-doubt threatens or rejection letters land in the mailbox. Our aim of bringing about a new worldview will fall short of the mark if we simply point people toward the goal of an antiracist, antioppressive world. For hope-filled action to lead to a cultural shift, we must create environments that help advocates for change stay engaged.

Empowering individuals and groups to resist the status quo is easier said than done. I believe powerful learning experiences that keep learners engaged over time are defined by a cocktail of hope, insight, and the skills to put them to use. In addition, the environment must allow results to be tested. Education theorist Joan Wink, in *Critical Pedagogy*, suggests that social change requires the ability to "learn, unlearn, and relearn" narratives that shape the stories we tell about ourselves, the stories we tell about others, and how we make meaning of the stories that are told about us. For example, she learned as a child that a positive way to understand American culture was through the metaphor of a melting pot. Later she had to unlearn that idea because, as she puts it, people at the bottom of the pot got burned. Wink writes that we must reshape these unhelpful stories in ways that move us forward with a more informed perspective.

Unlearning and relearning, however, cannot be done in a context that doesn't support growth. Transformation requires people to give up old ways of making meaning in order for new ways to take hold. In a study of classroom teachers deeply committed to changing the intellectual and social conditions of disempowered children, Jennifer Garvey Berger, in her article "Dancing on the Threshold of Meaning," tracked the sense of loss among teachers who unlearned and relearned the deeply held assumptions that shaped their commitments to social change in their classrooms and schools. Paradigmatic shifts—shattering the foundations of what we know and believe to be true and good—are significant events. Indeed, Berger writes, they "require that someone changes not just *what* she thinks but *how* she thinks about things. Such a change can lead people to see things they had not previously noticed, and to have choices they didn't realize they had." Berger says these shifts happen when individuals realize that a big assumption that once shaped their thinking no longer holds sway. They begin to "dance on the edge" of what they know to be true. As the teachers she studied moved away from certainty, they showed increased levels of fear and anxiety and were generally unable to conceptualize a way out of their muddle. At this moment of precious dissonance, when individuals can freely consider a new point of view, Berger suggests that they have enormous potential to expand the frames of reference that shape their lives. More important than the addition of new knowledge or understanding, this provides a new framework for making decisions and weighing commitments. This type of change, over time, represents the best hope for the social change we dream of seeing in our congregations and society. It enables us to model the kind of transformation we want to see in the world.

We need to understand how educators can create learning experiences that help people unlearn and relearn their skills and justice habits. I can recall one example from personal experience. Several years ago, I was asked to lead a seminar on transformative learning for students socialized into a white identity. A core objective of the seminar included helping this all-white group unveil how whiteness shaped their lives by making visible the influences and values shaping their worldview. My previous experience working with privileged groups taught me that a head-on approach (especially as a person of color leading this seminar) can sometimes cause more defensiveness than honest reflection. Asking white-identified people to name their identities, for example, often results in furrowed brows and puzzled expressions. Although there are always exceptions, many men socialized into whiteness tend to experience my seminars as "touchy-feely" reflective exercises, where they suspect me of playing a game that will frame them as Exhibit A: The Problematic White Male. Deciding to take a more humane approach, I asked the group to consider and identify "deeply felt characteristics at the core of your lives, so much so, that if those elements were eliminated, you would miss the point of your lives, you would not be yourselves." I then asked them to draw or chart these aspects of their identity. By asking this question, I learned as much about my own sense of righteousness as I did about how they engage with their own identity. Most of the men in the group were avid fans of the Boston Red Sox and wrote and spoke at length about how the core of their identities was shaped by the highs and lows of Red Sox season.

I became indignant. I wanted them to understand me, as a person whose physical, emotional, and spiritual identities are constantly on the margin. I wanted them to "get me," to voice how their lives were in direct contradiction to mine. If they could really see me for who I am, it could lead to some sort of reconciliation.

That recognition could signal "you matter" and "I feel your pain." Among facilitators of color, I suspect I am not alone in having this goal. When this group identified a sports team as being at the core of their identity, my first response was anger. How dare they equate the loss of a baseball game to the exploitation and discrimination that a gay man of color experiences in this world? Thankfully, I took a breath, became curious, and listened to the complex constructions of their identity—how their emotional and loving relationships with their fathers and grandfathers, for example, was nested in the context of Red Sox baseball. I realized that I had found a way to engage both of our growing edges. I did not devalue the fact that their point of entry into the world of identity politics was baseball and mine was sexual orientation and "race." After all, why should I expect them to connect—much less reconcile—with something far outside their own experience? Instead, in that moment, I created an opportunity for them to identify what makes their human story significant. As the seminar unfolded, I was able to help them construct meaning about how issues of "race" and gender and sexual orientation also inform their lives. In the end, they understood not only me and themselves but also how systems of socialization and oppression function. The exercise enabled us to collectively teeter on the edge of what we understood to be true, and in that moment, to push out our boundaries in order to develop capacity for a broader conception of human experience.

This story suggests that we should revisit how we structure educational events intended to foster deep change. Educators often valorize their experiences of eliciting such "aha" moments, celebrating in side conversations those moments when learners finally got it. Simply inducing those moments, however, differs from instilling fundamental changes in thought and behavior. John Dewey suggests in *Art as Experience* that for an experience to reach its deepest impact, it must be "integrated within and demarcated in the general stream of experience from other experiences." At a protest march, for example, some participants may be moved by the passion of song and speech but soon afterward revert to the very ways of thinking that they rallied against. Dewey's insight suggests that for these people, the "aha" moment is disconnected from the stream of experience that marks how they think and feel. When experience connects to and extends meaning-making, people are more likely to deepen their commitment to the issue at hand. The experience both challenges and supports these people. They find it attractive enough to call them to dance on the boundary of what they know to be true and robust enough to serve as a launching point for future discovery.

All of this suggests that educating for social justice requires us to create catalytic moments when new observations promote deeper self-knowledge or group knowledge. At the same time, it must encourage future growth, normalize ambiguity, and foster comfort in dancing on the edge of a new paradigm. Equally important, we educators must be attuned to our assumptions and to how our own needs and outlooks influence others' abilities to learn and grow on their own terms.

In sum, social justice scholars and practitioners must first pay more attention to the learning experience—its nature, how it happens, how it deepens and extends, and how to best facilitate it. Part of the horrible legacy of education in the U.S. context is the tendency to treat learners as objects to be manipulated or, worse yet, opponents to be worn down with compelling evidence. Perhaps, especially for adult learners, even benevolent imposition of our own thoughts, emotions, and perspectives can dam new streams of thought rather than open them. We must instead facilitate students' own experiences.

Second, equal attention must be paid to the tender work of skill building. Unlearning and relearning is deeply counterintuitive, as it requires discounting truths held with great affection and loyalty. Metanarratives of supremacy, competition, monoculturalism, either-or dualisms, and individuality must be interrupted and corrected by building hard-won skills.

Finally, while the story of the crab provides a powerful image of the individual struggle to become vulnerable in the midst of danger, the metaphor falls apart because it fails to capture the communal nature of educating for social justice. Our natural inclination to prefer certain ways of thinking—as well as our limited perspective on any given truth—demand that we always partner, collaborate, and cooperate with others. Educators and activists constantly move through dangerous waters, each of us vulnerable in differing ways. We must develop a philosophical and theological framework that, when nested in intentional communities of learning, allows sufficient space for hope coupled with action to work its metamorphosis.

The Pause That Refreshes

ALIDA DeCOSTER

Throughout my years as a parish minister, spiritual director, and searching human, I have learned the necessity of balancing action and reflection. Our work can be more effective, and we can be more enduring, if we create a particular kind of support structure for our efforts. At the Unitarian Universalist Washington Office for Advocacy, social justice interns work hard on Capitol Hill promoting peace and justice positions of the UUA and our General Assembly, yet every week we set aside time for group theological reflection. The sessions are theological in the personal sense: We reflect on the values and meanings inherent in our daily experiences.

Regular time for sharing our feelings and hopes and deepening our relationships is healing and refreshing. While these sessions do help prevent individual burnout, they also serve a deeper purpose: They develop our faith and deepen our work. As Thomas Merton wrote in *Contemplation in a World of Action*, "The one who attempts to act and do things for others or for the world without deepening his own self-understanding, freedom, integrity and capacity to love, will not have anything to give others."

The balance of action and reflection is reflected in the new UUA slogan: "Nurture your spirit, help heal our world." This captures the yin and yang of the spiritual life in one phrase. The deeper we can reach inside, the farther we can reach out. The more we can admit our own limitations and failings, forgive ourselves, and be healed, the more we grow in our compassion and calling as healers.

UUs often prefer to stay in the intellectual realm rather than risk facing the mystery and uncertainty within, yet a complete religious life must involve mind, heart, and body—the whole of us. The most important thing I learned from the 2005 Spiritual Guidance Program of the Shalem Institute in Bethesda, Maryland, was how to strengthen my heart orientation. Heart times of prayer and reflection enrich the journey and strengthen us to meet the call of justice. We need not abandon reason; it is one of our great strengths. We only need to supplement it with a deepening practice.

At the convocation in Baltimore that gave rise to this book, I was struck by the contrast between the first four sessions and the fifth. The first four sessions were excellent and challenging; the fifth took us to a whole new level. In a spontaneous presentation led by Paula Cole Jones, people of color spoke from their own experiences in UU settings. They spoke from their own experiences in UU settings. I found it both humbling and transformative. Structured like a theological reflection group, the session presented honest personal stories that took us to a deeper place, from head to heart—a place of fewer defenses and a greater likelihood of transformation. It should have been the first workshop.

At times I have been discouraged by the tendency of UUs to see personal spirituality as contradictory to the life of social activism. Spiritual discipline has been considered navel gazing, but all the great traditions proclaim the link between the inner life and the outer life. Some of history's greatest social justice leaders have been spiritual exemplars: Dorothy Day, Martin Luther King, Jr., and Gandhi. Those with the deepest faith, the strongest relationship with the divine, are those willing to take the greatest risks. Theirs is a faith that transcends life and death. We can learn from studying these lives and emulating them within our UU framework.

In Washington DC, hundreds of secular nonprofits share our commitments, including reproductive freedom, peace, civil rights, and economic justice. Yet the UUA Washington Office has a somewhat different orientation to its work. While secular organizations focus solely on their agenda, faith-based organizations like ours look at the origin of our views—our faith in the human spirit, our respect for the right of conscience, our reverence for nature, and the teachings of world religions. We are grounded not in issues of the day but in faith, love, and compassion for the long term. As individuals, we know our own capacity for evil, including the evil of ignorance, and our humility deepens our compassion. Rather than focusing on the other side, we stay open to creative solutions and patiently work for transformation we may not live to see. From this stance, we can be in strong solidarity with our companions—even those with whom we differ about the details—and we can rejoice in the triumph of justice when and where it happens. It helps to take the long view and realize that we have actually come a long way.

There is another way theological reflection groups can be helpful. Many UUs drop out of our social justice enterprise because they feel there is only one politically correct position on issues. In our congregations, we could form groups for those quietly struggling with perspectives they fear are unacceptable in the broader UU community. An example I heard involved an older person not comfortable with marriage equality for gay, lesbian, bisexual, and transgender people. That opinion might never change if there is no place for understanding and engagement between those with differing views of these fast-moving social changes. Do we really affirm diversity of opinion? And are opinions unshakable? Most people who are grounded in compassion and informed through personal stories come to recognize injustice. This is certainly true for me. How many more issues are still beneath my own radar? Mutual acceptance, authentic dialogue, and forgiveness of ourselves and one another must always be central to our spiritual lives. Without the conversations they engender, we cannot make progress.

At the conference, we were called to accountability by the final set of speakers. Engaging in authentic relationships across racial, ethnic, and class lines is challenging. We are only beginning to develop ourselves this way as a movement. As Paula Cole Jones said that day, the situation is urgent, and the core of the work is reconciliation. Unitarian Universalism must catch up or fade away. We must speak to each other from a deeper place, and we must listen more than speak.

In white people's antiracism and antioppression work and in white allies groups—recognizing that historically marginalized groups should not have to do all the educating themselves—the soul work that we engage in must involve confession and forgiveness in order to reach new levels of awareness. We will stumble and make mistakes. We must be able to move through our own sense of confusion and our fears to serve the vision of our faith. I hope that we can develop a model of ongoing groups for support in this work.

It will be useful to have some guidelines for theological reflection in congregational and other groups, based on the practice of the Washington Office. Many of our churches have embraced small-group ministry in the last decade, and that model is easily adapted for this purpose. In fact, the structure of the Washington Office group is similar to that of a covenant group. Social justice committees can also designate some meetings for reflection, or they can break into smaller groups or dyads for checking in.

At the Washington Office, we begin with a chalice lighting and opening words, often followed by a period of silence (as the Quakers know, the deep listening that can happen in silence is often easier in a group than on one's own). As they check in, the interns openly share the events of their lives, and bonding naturally takes place. Guidelines of confidentiality increase the degree that participants feel they can trust each other with personal information.

The personal check-in is followed by some kind of story or program. This piece has often been a challenge in covenant groups. In our setting, we brainstorm about twelve topics at a time and schedule them for upcoming meetings. Typically, once the presentation is made, there is another time for sharing our responses or similar experiences, followed by a closing meditation or reading. We have started a practice of passing the chalice for joys and concerns at the end of the meeting. Although books can be used for content—and we have gained much from Rebecca Parker's *Blessing the World*, Marjorie Bowens-Wheatley and Nancy Palmer Jones's *Soul Work*, and Paul Rasor's *Faith without Certainty*, among others—we are wary of depending on written words, for they tend to give rise to a discussion experience that circumvents deeper sharing. Each month, we dedicate one session to an issue that the office is addressing. Our director or associate director leads this session with information about UU history, General Assembly resolutions, and Statements of Conscience.

In all these sessions, participants share individually, without cross talk, and speak about their feelings on an issue or experience. If there is time, we move to a general discussion, but doing so too quickly forfeits the remarkable depth and growth that comes from taking time for individual sharing.

Those who have led covenant group programs know the variations that are possible in this format, depending on the situation and sense of the facilitator. The key is to be explicit that the group is a support for social justice ministry. In addition, the facilitator must have had some training in leadership and group dynamics and must be overseen by a minister or someone with a similar skill set.

A personal story related to social justice ministry is a good way to begin theological reflection. Another possibility, when participants are actively involved in particular social justice projects, is to invite them to speak of successes and frustrations with that work. With young adult interns, I have found that stories about experiences of injustice in their own lives can be a great starting point, as can general topics such as power in relationships, human emotions, or careers in social justice. We have reflected on the apocalypse, had water communions, prepared for and debriefed after General Assembly, watched films, heard speakers, and gone on field trips. Overall, it is the group's intimacy that leads to deepening and growth. Intimacy can emerge from being together all day, every day, as it does in our setting, or from ongoing relationships over time, as in a parish.

UUs can learn from Christianity in this practice. Though I am a lifelong UU, I have been transformed by my exposure to the Christian contemplative tradition, which showed me that the more we meet the divine within, the more we can bring that divinity forth. Kenneth Leech puts it so well in his book *True Prayer*:

> Our path is one of exploration *into* God, an exploration which involves a real transformation of the personality. Such a transformation is the goal of human history, and it must include both the personal and the political. There can be no genuine transformation in the political order without a profound change in individual consciousness. But equally there can be no personal change which does not carry with it the demand for radical change in society.

Leech expresses my conviction that social justice work must be accompanied by honest and searching inner work, which eventually leads to a realization of universal love and our belonging in the universe. This awareness compels us to serve. I hope that we can develop a model of this twin enterprise—inner work and outer work—and my experience shows that theological reflection groups can help to do this.

Growing Our Souls

PAULA COLE JONES

I draft this essay as a letter to Unitarian Universalists, past, present, and future.

A decade ago, I received a request from my home congregation, All Souls Church, Unitarian, in Washington DC, to help them begin a process of reconciliation after conflict and the termination of a minister who was African American. The situation left the church in a state of racial angst. Since then, change and justice in Unitarian Universalist congregations have been at the center of my personal, professional, and spiritual life. Recently, I was invited to accompany William Sinkford, then president of the Unitarian Universalist Association, on a spiritual pilgrimage to Africa, which included learning about the work of the Truth and Reconciliation Commission in South Africa. I hope my reflections on these last ten years contribute to contemporary UU understanding of prophetic congregations.

I cannot imagine engaging with Unitarian Universalism without its justice and multiculturalism components. As a person of color, I would have little purpose for voluntarily spending my time in an institution not engaged in an examination of these issues. The history of inequality and oppression is too long and too troubling to tolerate indifference to the ways that these forces affect people, regardless of whether the inequity is an advantage or disadvantage. Racism and oppression are constantly in play, and they gain power through our silence. The absence of a conversation about race does not mean that racism is not operating, but the silence makes it harder to hold people accountable for making change to the structures that have historically supported inequities.

I am a lifelong UU, who grew up in a prophetic congregation. At All Souls Church, the principles and values of Unitarian Universalism were imprinted on my soul in a congregation that crossed the barriers of race. Had the church not diligently worked on racial inclusion, I doubt it would have met my needs. For me, there is no separation between Unitarian Universalism and antiracism, antioppression, and multiculturalism.

The prophetic church has many roles. It does the difficult work of truth and reconciliation, and sets a new course that calls people to a higher level of discourse and humanity. It casts a vision that illuminates the way like a beam of light and calls us to walk with fellow travelers and together build a new reality. The prophetic church equips us for the journey, fortifies our courage, stokes our passion, rekindles our flame, and supports the community in the process. It reinvents itself and a piece of the world by bringing into being justice and compassion. Public opinion and future generations will recognize it as prophetic.

A prophetic leader does not make a prophetic congregation. While all ministers and congregations would like to be seen as prophetic, truly prophetic congregations build the collective commitment necessary to power personal and social transformation. There is a large gap between intellectually understanding the need to work for justice and transformation and actively working to do so. Until we face the truth about racism and about the social construction of identity—as well as systems that support social hierarchy and inequality—we will likely produce flawed social change that only reinforces white privilege.

My ability to see truth and reconciliation as at the core of justice ministries was sharpened during my trip to Africa in November 2008. I traveled there with Sinkford and his wife, Maria; Eric Cherry,

UUA director of international relations; and Bruce Knotts, director of the UU United Nations Office. We began our trip in South Africa, the setting of one of the most dramatic stories of injustice and truth and reconciliation in our lifetimes. It would be too easy to glorify the accomplishments there as though justice was served and the past can now be left in the past. This is not the case. One of the most effective outcomes of the truth and reconciliation process has been the representation of the past in art. Museums, murals, and monuments tell stories of those who have called South Africa home, from the oldest population of modern humans on Earth to those involved in the evils of colonialism and white supremacy under apartheid. As one of the Truth and Reconciliation commissioners, Mary Burton, said, "South Africa may have succeeded at truth, but reconciliation has not been achieved yet."

The necessity of societal truth telling is one of the most powerful lessons that I bring back from my journey. We should be cautious when congratulating ourselves for doing justice if we have not done the soul-stirring work of uncovering the truth and hearing the human tragedy of injustice. The purpose of working toward social change is not only to solve problems but also to realize our common humanity.

The prophetic church presents a vision that compels us to act. The vision enables leaders not only to see future possibilities but to identify barriers and obstacles to their fulfillment. On October 1, 2008, the UUA Leadership Council adopted a vision statement for Unitarian Universalism in a multicultural world:

> With humility and courage born of our history, we are called as Unitarian Universalists to build the Beloved Community where all souls are welcome as blessings, and the human family lives whole and reconciled.

Change requires strong leadership, and certain strategies can enable leaders to be more effective in inspiring their congregations. As I conducted multicultural competency assessments with UU leaders over the past few years, I recognized a pattern: A majority of leaders rate themselves high on multicultural competencies and their congregations low. Whether or not people are as far along as they think, personal competencies are not translating into leadership in congregational life.

Congregational leaders are up against the attitudes and baggage of congregants. Since confronting this inertia can lead to burnout, the very people who work to build momentum toward cultural and systemic change are ones most likely to leave. Leaders must develop strategies for staying focused and inspired. One strategy is to connect with a group of leaders in antiracism, antioppression, and multicultural efforts outside one's own church to form a challenging and inspiring learning community. For example, my early engagement with my district transformation team helped to keep me from giving up.

Although my congregation has long been committed to multiculturalism, board members were unsettled by antiracism. We provided annual Jubilee II antiracism workshops to groom new leaders and retool existing ones. Boards rarely take the lead in this work, but systemic change is easier when they do. Inadequate preparation of new members can lead to a loss of momentum. After five or seven years, we knew we were at a turning point when new board members assumed their positions already trained in antiracism. In 2001, when Robert Hardies was still new to his ministry, his embrace of antiracism helped to make it widely accepted at All Souls Church, and the momentum shifted in favor of change.

There is no doubt that ministers are key to unlocking the power of justice ministries, and to helping congregations work on dealing with privilege, racism, and oppression. A minister who leads a congregation in facing these challenges and transforming itself is likely to capture the attention of people who see the congregation as prophetic because it achieves what others find difficult or would not attempt at all.

A prophetic minister cannot create a prophetic congregation without the commitment of a critical mass of members. Under congregational polity, freedom of the pulpit blesses prophetic ministers with a platform, but the congregation's power to call and terminate ministers can make ministers hesitant to take risks that would make some congregants uncomfortable. The prophetic minister who runs into trouble with a congregation that is not ready for change may have a short-lived ministry with that church. However, even a failed attempt to build a critical mass of people supporting change may educate the congregation and increase the odds that change will follow. If the truth and reconciliation process can be applied in these situations, tremendous growth can result, slowly restoring the emotional and spiritual health of all involved.

Collective commitment is stronger if it consists of both individual and public engagement. Building commitment and a critical mass takes time. I have seen people hold out for years before stepping into the work of antiracism. Congregants may resent the notion that they have work to do in accepting people regardless of their identities. However, we must all retool ourselves to meet the demands of justice and inclusion in the new millennium. If we already knew enough about these problems, why would they persist? Collective commitment is an intellectual, spiritual, emotional, and physical act. It is a spiritual task to humble ourselves and lower our defenses long enough to find our connection to the issue and to each other.

I want UUs to shift our language from *social justice* to *social change*. It is too easy to merely talk about social justice; social change requires more. Educator Jonathan Kozol writes about "systemic justice rather than seasonal philanthropy." How much of our work is seasonal philanthropy? Social change requires empowered people, change agents who know when to follow and when to lead, and groups willing to work against injustice long enough to get results. How strong is our faith? Are we up for the challenges? Is our collective vision stronger than the problems we face?

David H. Eaton, the first African-American minister of All Souls Church, addressed the challenge of speaking about versus being a just, beloved community:

> The most persistent problem in American life has been the gap between the values espoused and the values observed. . . . The real road to reconciliation will be a bumpy road. . . . It will deal with the dream deferred with the same determination that it presently deals with being number one. I believe with every sinew of my being that the first society that builds its priorities on the disinherited will be the first universal society. . . . Then we will understand that when we do it for the least of our brothers, we do it for ourselves.

Justice brought about through social change will change us in the process.

The UU Church of Riverside, California, was reenergized when it began to address the problem of homelessness in its community. The congregation's work with JUUST Change consultant John Gilmore to understanding racism and linked oppressions prepared its members to work across racial and class barriers. Within seven months, the congregation had gained new life through this justice ministry. Its work evolved from the seasonal philanthropy of preparing and delivering hygiene kits to social change through reorienting itself to the systemic issues that caused injustice. Several members of the church joined the mayor's task force on homelessness and advocated for affordable housing with state legislators. The church partnered with members of the homeless community and became a census center for identifying homeless people.

The First Unitarian Society (FUS) of Madison, Wisconsin, one of the largest UU congregations, has very few members who are people of color, yet it has become a strong partner in addressing the achievement gap between students of color and white students in local public schools. Wendy Cooper, the social justice coordinator at FUS, said that education is core to Madison's identity, but African-American high school students' graduation rate there is 60 percent less than that of white students (who perform well above the national average). To address this issue, some educators began to use African-centered pedagogy to engage and retain African-American students. The program was terminated by the school administration, with no plan to address the graduation problem. Representatives of an African Methodist Episcopal church asked Cooper what FUS might do to help. Working through the interfaith group Dane County United, Cooper brought the support of this large congregation and twenty-two other white churches to the partnership. The school system not only restored the programs but provided significant funding for expansion. Cooper noted that this change "will affect the quality of life for the larger community in the years to come."

The past decade has seen the passing of a generation of people who embodied a commitment to social change, among them my mother, Betty Cole; Marjorie Bowens Wheatley; and many others, longtime UUs and allies in the struggle for justice working in multicultural communities. However, there is cause for optimism in the coming of age of young people who have been raised on UU values of justice and inclusion.

The task of prophetic ministry is to break out of unjust socially conditioned beliefs so that we do not pass them on to another generation, saddling them with work that is ours to do. My own daughter, Kendall, who at twenty-five years old is a student of social and cultural history, is much better prepared for the task than I was at her age. Each generation is called to reconsider old beliefs, fashion new ones, and contribute to humankind. As young people enter the adult world and UU ministry, the clarity of their vision will change things.

A prophetic minister of a prophetic congregation, A. Powell Davies of All Souls Church, once said, "Life is just a chance to grow a soul." We have not finished growing our souls. The growth of our souls is reflected in our congregations and in the power of our partnerships in the community. Open yourself to change. Be courageous. Commit to the struggle to reconcile injustice and embrace the multicultural community.

Come Ye Disconsolate

TAQUIENA BOSTON

Maybe because I was born in the same year as *Brown v. Board of Education*, I have always known that brokenness is not only individual but social and collective. Religious community and theology so often hold a people struggling with brokenness, suffering, and injustice. My earliest influences in being held this way are my family church and the movement for African-American civil rights.

At Saint Paul African Methodist Episcopal Church in Washington DC, where I grew up, the hymn "Come Ye Disconsolate" called worshipers to the altar for personal prayer:

Come ye disconsolate, where're ye languish
Come to the mercy seat, fervently kneel
Here bring your wounded heart, here tell your anguish
Earth hath no sorrow that heaven cannot heal

Established as the E Street Mission in southwest Washington in 1856, Saint Paul has a history inseparable from abolitionism and the struggle for racial equality. The congregation's founding minister, Anthony Bowen, formed the first YMCA for colored men in 1853. The church served as a stop on the Underground Railroad. Bowen joined Frederick Douglass and John F. Cook Jr. to recruit the first black regiment from Washington DC, the First U.S. Colored Troops, in 1863. After the Civil War, he petitioned the mayor to provide free public education for African-American children on the grounds that blacks were taxpaying citizens.

I hesitated to write about Saint Paul in a Unitarian Universalist context for two reasons: first, because the congregation cannot defend itself against my memory; second, because in order to accurately re-create that memory I must resort to the religious language of the Saint Paul community and risk being dismissed by members of my chosen faith. Although I discovered Unitarian Universalism as a young adult more than twenty years ago and feel it has always been my authentic religious identity, I have often had to navigate border spaces as culturally other in my faith community and religiously other in the African-American community. However, I cannot speak about faith, brokenness, suffering, and injustice without crossing back and forth between these communities and their theologies.

Despite its history, I would not label Saint Paul in the 1960s and 1970s an activist church. It was the congregation where Uncle Johnny volunteered with the Boosters Club, Cousin Dorothy supervised the Sunday School, and Cousin Earl cooked the meals that bridged the time between the morning worship and the afternoon fund raisers. Saint Paul was the place where our community's families marked all the important rituals from birth to death. The church had no committees for social justice or community outreach. However, like many historically black congregations, Saint Paul played an important role in supporting the African-American community materially and spiritually.

My earliest image of how faith holds a people in brokenness and suffering is Saint Paul members walking down the sunlit aisles in the former synagogue to bring their wounded hearts, anguish, sorrow, and loss to the wide wooden altar, as the choir sang "Come Ye Disconsolate." Those prayerful moments in the church demonstrated the equality of all in the eyes of the Creator: school teachers and nurses, government workers and college professors, beauticians and truck drivers, domestics and day laborers—all came to kneel humbly in private conversation with their God. When they rose to return to the pews, their eyes sometimes held tears but always held hope, and their bodies were outlined by the glow from stained glass windows, still decorated with Stars of David.

Saint Paul, the extended family of a congregation made up of extended families, gave aid and comfort in times of trouble. The pastor, deacons, and missionary sisters connected individual families and the congregation. The first to find out about illness, death, or family catastrophe, they visited the sick and shut-in, sat with the bereaved, cooked and cleaned for people recovering from surgery, and became surrogate family for members with no other relatives to care for them. The church family assisted with funeral arrangements and collected clothes, food, money, or whatever was needed to help members in hard times. Extending service to those in need was evidence of what it meant to be Christian.

The congregation extended its care and comfort beyond the membership to welcome the stranger, recruiting neighborhood children for Sunday school and vacation Bible school. Adults groomed youth in the ways of doing church: worshiping, ushering, singing in the choir, fund raising, and leading Bible lessons. They consciously instilled pride and affirmed racial and religious identity in a city stratified by race, color, and class, not only between blacks and whites but also within the black community.

In the 1960s, social status in Washington was communicated not only by race and ethnicity but also through education, profession, material assets, and physical appearance. As early as age four, I saw that children with fair skin and silky hair were viewed as more attractive, intelligent, and well behaved by black and white society. I recognized that the black proprietor of my nursery school had great respect for the children whose parents worked for the federal government and owned their houses and that she treated me indifferently because my mother worked at a laundry, my father worked for a trash company, and we rented the upstairs apartment in another family's home. I went to an all-black elementary school, where the white principal did not allow teachers to give A's to students because she was convinced of the inferiority of black people. Aunts, uncles, and neighbors, when moved by television images of attack dogs and fire hoses turned on students and marchers, told personal stories about unfair treatment at work, in stores, by police, or while traveling through white neighborhoods.

The church, while not immune from race, color, and class discrimination, provided fortification for struggling against racial and economic injustice. Ministers in the 1960s and 1970s would never use a word like *empowerment*, but it was the subtext of sermons and the Bible stories they most frequently referenced. They spoke of evil as a social condition that was evident in oppression and inequality. The sermons about oppression came clothed in stories of persecuted prophets and other Biblical protagonists with whom the congregation could identify, those ancient stories often paired with accounts of contemporary civil rights struggles.

The church asserted that neither material assets nor profession nor social standing determined intrinsic worth. God conferred worth and dignity. No matter the struggles and injustice in the world, the faithful would find support in times of trouble. The righteous will not be forsaken, we were told. The meek shall inherit the earth. We shall overcome. Earth hath no sorrow that heaven cannot heal. These messages gave me a strong sense of my own possibilities despite the larger society's messages.

As much as the Saint Paul community formed my understanding of how theology holds brokenness and suffering, the most influential minister of my childhood and early youth was a Baptist minister from Georgia. Martin Luther King, Jr., spoke to the brokenness and suffering caused by injustice in society. His words, echoing the messages I heard from the pulpit, named injustice and oppression as evils that had to be transformed—but King went further. He called the oppressor as well as the oppressed to a vision of beloved community, a society of love and justice that all people were responsible for creating.

When King expanded his ministry and advocacy to include work for peace, antipoverty, and economic justice, I realized that social justice is ever evolving and that the work of making justice is never done. King's ministry underscored religious teachings that the core of faith was not what people believed but how they lived their values. Religious people face a difficult challenge: not choosing between compassion and justice but learning how the two can operate together. Neither compassion alone nor justice in the form of retribution can heal the brokenness caused by injustice and oppression. King taught that justice unified with compassion is the supreme demonstration of love.

As I witnessed King's work at the intersection of his religious identity and social justice, I unconsciously absorbed the wisdom that living as a person of faith means practicing social justice. And I learned that one role of the church is to support its members in acting justly beyond its walls. However, a time came when the support that Saint Paul offered was inadequate to hold the identity struggles I experienced as a working-class, first-generation college student. Although the congregation continued to affirm me with positive messages, the theology did not address the complexity that I witnessed in worlds beyond the church community. However, the college environment lacked the values that I cherished at Saint Paul, as well as its emphasis on integrity and character.

My search for something to anchor me led me to other theologies. At the Howard University School of Religion library, I immersed myself in the philosophies of Howard Thurman, Zen Buddhists, existentialists, and Christian mystics, as well as traditions of the Far East, to help me cope with my personal anguish. Though the philosophies provided useful insights, they did not provide comfort. I found myself listening a lot to "Come Ye Disconsolate," as recorded by Donny Hathaway and Roberta Flack. Many years later I commented to a Unitarian Universalist friend that it would have been helpful to know about Unitarian Universalism during that difficult time because it is a faith where questions are respected as part of the spiritual journey.

When I discovered Unitarian Universalism a decade later, as a young adult at All Souls Church, Unitarian, in Washington DC, I found a faith with justice at its core. I did not leave Saint Paul because I rejected anything; I joined All Souls because Unitarian Universalism was theologically expansive, included more social identities, emphasized human agency, and brought together faith and justice. For many years, All Souls was the religious home that fortified me through all the disappointing presidential elections, irrational wars, and halting progress of social justice movements. Unitarian Universalism challenged me to continue to expand my consciousness of the ways that injustice manifests in human relationships—not only with regard to race, gender, and class but also sexual orientation, disability, age, nationality, and religion.

My childhood religion still holds me, but in a different way. I understand the messages of empowerment as visible evidence of a people's capacity to endure and to create beauty in music, expressive worship, and in the many acts of service to families and their communities. There are times when I need to culturally immerse myself in the historically black church and hear the fortifying messages of my childhood, especially at times when events affecting the larger African-American community produce occasions of mourning or celebration.

The 2008 U.S. election pushed my buttons on race, class, and gender issues, and I found myself having, not a "come-to-Jesus" moment, but a "come-to-the-chalice" moment. Intellectually, I knew that the United States was having identity encounters, and the presidential primaries and election confronted people with identity issues about which many were either unconscious or in denial. Remnants of historical racism, classism, sexism, and heterosexism asserted themselves strongly. Emotionally, I was scared—not afraid, but *scared*—of what I might learn about the only country I could truly call home, despite my desire to be a citizen of the planet. All of my family was here in the United States, and my known ancestors had been in Virginia for more than two hundred years. Education and profession had taken me to new class territory, but geographically I had not traveled far from my ancestors' home.

Increasingly, I needed a local religious community that would support me in being faithful to the vision and values of the beloved community—the community of love and justice—no matter the outcome of the general election. Even after the election, I knew that the United States did not enter the promised land on November 4, but stood on the boundary of the next struggle for social justice. The realization became a decision to renew my connection with a Unitarian Universalist congregation. My mature faith requires a community that will challenge my social consciousness, ground my commitment to justice in compassion, and nurture me spiritually by supporting me in living the values of love and justice.

Unitarian Universalism is my religious home. It is not a perfect faith community for a woman of color from a working-class family. Our congregations' struggle to be fully racially and culturally inclusive is a continuing source of disappointment, and it is painful to admit that not all social identities find full welcome in our faith. Despite the tensions and contradictions between Unitarian Universalists' principles and practices, in matters of faith and social justice I find in it a more expansive altar where I can bring my wounded heart and tell my anguish.

Not for Ourselves Alone

CAROL CAOUETTE

Sunday morning, 9 a.m.: Rev. Victoria Safford swirls a leather wand around and around a large crystal singing bowl, generating a hum that fills the sanctuary—a mellow G below middle C pulled from the air, the tone of the voice chakra. The hum of the bowl plays with the acoustics, literally setting the tone of the room. Now we are invited to hear every sound that will flow through the sanctuary this morning. Now we are ready to give full voice to the hymns, chants, and words that awe will sing and say aloud in community.

As the service proceeds, I steal occasional glances around the room. I want to look at all the faces, curious to know what everyone is feeling. What is moving others? Are they moved in the same way I am? Are we connecting? Seated at the piano, I hear reactions to musical pieces: wows, sighs, ahs, and sniffles. I see tears, joy, calm, and a singular kind of unselfconsciousness. This is all part of the experience of the hour as we sit in sanctuary, affirming our worth, checking in with one another, worshiping in our unique ways, together. These are the holy moments we share, held in trust by those who weave the service with intention and attention. We worship and sing together in community, seeking inspiration not only for ourselves but for the social justice work that we so passionately pursue.

At White Bear Unitarian Universalist Church in the little hamlet of Mahtomedi, Minnesota, an eclectic array of creative Unitarian Universalists, amateur and professional, are inspired to use their art to make a difference. Congregants find that the challenges of artistic and musical collaboration help them grow personally and help others in the congregation experience joy and contemplation deeply linked to one another's lives and interests. Music and art take us into unfamiliar territory; we give each other permission to experiment, playing with the space in the safety of sanctuary walls. Choral and ensemble music ranges from classical pieces to traditional gospel music, the tone from contemplative to rollicking. The more eclectic, the more inclusive. Member songwriters and composers offer new or rearranged compositions; new musical collaborations are continuously imagined, adding yet another new voice to the mix.

Planning worship and events collaboratively becomes intuitive with practice. The seed of an idea germinates in several minds at once, and suddenly elements mesh into cohesive worship, social action, or fund-raising. The hard work of logistics and details follows once the roots take hold. The music director pores over musical texts and recordings, harvesting ideas and matching musicians, choral texts, and moods to the minister's theme. The minister uncovers and makes explicit the theme's connection to the music. Both minister and musician design service elements that evoke the season, the mood of the time, or even a recent joy or sorrow within the church community.

Service leaders and congregants alike do sacred and fierce work on Sunday mornings and in other ceremonies marking life passages. Attendees at a Sunday service arrive with particular histories, experiences, purposes, and needs. The simple, carefully prepared order of service only roughly guides the way we spend the hour together. Each person has a unique place among the readers, speakers, musicians, and congregants. A holistic, authentically moving experience, stirring us toward healing, change, and growth results from the leaders' focused intention. An authentic, high-quality experience in the sanctuary happens when we allow ourselves to be open to a communal encounter with the holy. We move from an awareness of our particular identities, concerns, and need to control to an unselfconscious meditative presence.

My understanding of this presence has deepened through the writing of Peter Senge and his collaborators. In the essay "Awakening Faith in an Alternative Future," their interviews with cutting-edge scientists, entrepreneurs, and artists led them to describe *presence* as a process of deep listening that moves us beyond preconceptions to a state of letting come. In Christianity, such a shift is called grace, revelation, or the Holy Spirit; in Taoism, *shin*; in Buddhism, cessation; in Hinduism, wholeness or oneness; in Sufism, an opening of the heart. We see and feel this shift on Sunday mornings when we practice listening deeply, without imposing analysis or images onto the music—when we practice letting it come.

Sanctuary time is relief from ordinary time. We are privileged to enjoy even a moment of sitting in a place of peace, receiving some spiritual nourishment. In a UU Musicians Network conference workshop on creating alternative, more inclusive services, Wayne Arnason and Kathleen Rolenz assigned special weight to Sunday service liturgy and music. They said that along with the sermon, music and liturgy should "rearrange the spirit." When the spirit is willing, a magical thing happens—hearts blossom and are suddenly available to feel extraordinary things. In the extraordinary we can see what is possible.

Music engenders an immediate and heartfelt experience of a spiritual community's unique voice. A stunning piece of music can electrify space, transform us emotionally, and propel us beyond our ordinary lives. The sanctuary becomes a crucible in which we mix an olio of words, music, and spirit to strengthen our collective voice. Communal singing connects us in immediate and visceral ways to each other and our times, refreshing and steeling us for our return to daily life. Through music and worship, congregations simultaneously honor and refashion tradition. Music and worship also lead us to new insights, which permeate our church life, including our justice work. They remind us that what can be imagined can often be realized.

Any work we do within our congregation is bound to affect our work outside its walls. Together we walk the journey of a church year full of free-ranging meditations, readings, music, prayers, and sermons. These elements give meaningful voice to our lives, reminding us of the circle of life and how we are connected. To nurture our communal voice into a prophetic one is to understand that we come from the same essence as the music and words from which we seek inspiration. Music and liturgy at their best resonate with the lives, cares, and concerns of the congregation. They remind us of our human connection. In community, we practice speaking, singing, and hearing the language of love and compassion—the transformative ingredients of social change.

A moving performance can communicate what it means to feel powerless or full of possibility. This was demonstrated on a recent October Sunday evening, when a choir of nearly a hundred voices sang passionately about hunger ("Famine Song"), the victims of Hurricane Katrina ("I've Been in the Storm So Long"), calls for action ("Can You Hear?"), and Shaker tunes about the personal search for peace, love, and salvation. The sixty-person adult choir of the congregation joined forces with the community choir Global Harmony to put on a benefit concert for Second Harvest Food Bank. The audience was small, but the free-will offering at the concert drew in six thousand dollars. It is hard to convey how soulfully persuasive the music of that evening was, but those in attendance had no doubt of it. The music moved people to give generously. Perhaps on this particular evening, we managed to experience together what it means to be alive in sacred time and space and once more remind ourselves that what can be imagined can often be realized.

When Love Speaks in Public

KATE LORE

I am often asked to explain the success of the social justice ministry of First Unitarian Church of Portland, Oregon. Unitarian Universalists around the country are surprised when they discover the size and scope of our work, and I end up fielding a fair number of calls and emails asking me to provide a set of best practices.

I wish that I could tell you that all a congregation needs to unleash its prophetic power is stirring sermons, passionate people, sacred engagement, and—*voila!*—the work will be set in motion. If this were the case, far more Unitarian Universalists churches would thrive in this country than do today, with far greater impact on public life. It is not enough to repeat a formula that is successful elsewhere.

Prophetic ministries are by their very nature contextual, relational, and dynamic, emerging when a congregation responds to an injustice experienced by community members who know and care about one another. Their shape is influenced by leadership style, mission, access to power and resources, demographics, patterns of oppression, theology, community partnerships, and more. Therefore, surveys of best practices hold little value in this arena. Justice is not to be achieved by following a set of best practices. In the words of Martin Luther King biographer Michael Eric Dyson, "Justice is what love looks like when it speaks in public."

We are an association of congregations free of any creed or doctrine, yet we have chosen to include these words in our hymnal:

Love is the doctrine of this church,
The quest of truth is its sacrament,
And service is its prayer.
To dwell together in peace,
To seek knowledge in freedom,
To serve human need,
To the end that all souls shall
Grow into harmony with the Divine—
Thus do we covenant with each other
And with God.

Many of us read these words aloud at every service, and they are prominently framed and hung in some of our buildings. These covenantal words are precious to our people, part of our Unitarian Universalist identity.

What is the nature of this love? In his first letter to the Corinthians, found in the New Testament of the Bible, the apostle Paul describes love as patient and kind, not jealous or boastful, not arrogant or rude or insistent on its own way, not irritable or resentful. Love rejoices in the right. "It bears all things, believes all things, hopes all things, endures all things."

This passage, often used in our celebrations of marriage and civil union, describes love's compassionate aspects, not those aspects of love we draw upon when encountering evil. Love does not guide us to be patient in the face of injustice or to endure any sort of systemic oppression, but it calls us together to challenge the status quo, to liberate the oppressed, and break the chains that bind us—all without succumbing to hate. Dr. Martin Luther King, Jr., spoke of these aspects of love when he wrestled with racism, economic injustice, and violence. In a sermon delivered at Dexter Avenue Baptist Church in Montgomery, Alabama, King said,

> In the final analysis, love is not this sentimental something that we talk about. It's not merely an emotional something.

> Love is creative. . . . It is the refusal to defeat any individual. When you rise to the level of love, of its great beauty and power, you seek only to defeat evil systems. Individuals who happen to be caught up in that system, you love, but you seek to defeat the system.

This is the love that fills our songs, inspires our readings, and emboldens our acts of social witness. It is divine, neither easy to practice nor easy to sustain. People lacking understanding of themselves or their role in the world's problems cannot embody its dynamic power. Prophetic love requires discipline, humility, and practice. Those who surrender their life to the work of love must strive for nonviolence, listen to many divergent voices, cultivate understanding among groups, and aggressively alter the systems that drive us apart. This is sacred work.

Love should be our guide in approaching conflict within our congregations. Unitarian theologian James Luther Adams said that church is where we learn how to be human. Congregations provide communal environments for discerning core commitments. With discernment, however, comes debate, and Unitarian Universalists often show a lack of love when debating, contributing to our lack of growth, in all senses of that word. We act as if congregations are academic rather than covenantal communities. Academic settings involve challenge and critique to hone intellectual capacity and develop unique ideas. Congregational settings, on the other hand, involve listening and connection to honor our whole beings and discover common purpose, shared yearnings, and unity with all life. This journey of the heart cannot go far in a competitive atmosphere.

A prophetic ministry spurs change and challenges resistance, yet it must also engage in conflict in ways that do not jeopardize relationships. Until we learn to approach conflict with love for our adversaries, we will never attain the change we seek. We must learn how to hold ourselves to standards worthy of our high aspirations and lofty goals.

The role of covenant is essential in prophetic churches. Over the past several decades, as Unitarian Universalists have challenged systems of oppression, we have made some positive impacts but also left a long trail of broken relationships around issues of race and class. Instead of covenants that will sit on shelves gathering dust, their relational implications forgotten, we need a working, living reminder of the conscientious people we aspire to be. Otherwise, our best intentions get derailed by pettiness, gossip, fear—all the human flaws that surface when tempers flare or egoism goes unchecked.

The covenant used by Social Justice Council of First Unitarian Church in Portland, Oregon, serves as the anchor of our ministry. It is effective because it places a high priority on love and relationships, the willingness to be vulnerable, the expectation of discipline, and the explicit inclusion of the need to forgive and be forgiven. It reads:

My Commitment as a Leader to Speak Truth with Love
I will communicate openly.
I will speak honestly and not withhold myself.
If I have a problem with someone, I will speak to the person, not about them.
I will speak clearly and concretely.
I will seek to understand, listening with an open heart and an open mind.
I will withhold judgment and check out my assumptions.
I will be open to feedback from others.
I will act with heart.
I will share how I feel as well as what I think.
I will bring my heart to painful issues.
I will be courteous to others, but not at the expense of speaking my truth.
I will treat others with respect, even when we disagree.
I will act with integrity.
I will take responsibility for what I say and do.

I will take personal responsibility to do my part for the well being of the group.
I will try to discern when to stick to principle and when to let go.
I will abide by agreements about disclosing information.
I will cultivate personal relationships.
I will approach others and myself with humor and joy.
I will seek to know others as people.
I will be friendly and welcoming.
I will acknowledge and appreciate others.
I will honor their contributions.
I will respect the requirements of unique roles.
I pledge to observe these practices, to do my best to trust that others are observing them, and to forgive others and myself when we inevitably make mistakes. I will hold others accountable and expect others to hold me accountable.

Hard conflicts arise in Portland's social justice ministry, as when our Racial Justice Committee members clashed with our Sunday School teachers or when our Peace Action group threatened to rip apart over the Israel-Palestine conflict. Some days the rage was so hot that some questioned whether they would ever be able to hold a loving thought toward their opponent again—and yet by continually calling themselves back to the covenant, they were able to resolve the conflict and heal the relationship.

Although I doubt anyone involved would care to repeat our experiences with conflict, most would agree that working through our struggles in the spirit of love fostered deeper understanding, mutual respect, and stronger relationships, thus strengthening the bonds that hold us together. We have grown spiritually as a result, and this, in turn, has enhanced the quality of our justice work.

That our program continues to thrive is a testament to the strength of our covenant. Conflict is inherent in justice work, so we return again and again to the promises we have made to one another, that we may teach one another how to be human.

We need those among us with people skills to lead our social justice efforts. While Unitarian Universalists generally spend a lot of time reflecting on and composing our congregational covenants, we often neglect to demonstrate similar wisdom when choosing people to lead our justice efforts. Most of us have experienced being cornered by people who passionately explain to us the details of the latest social injustice—regardless of whether we have the time or interest to hear them out. While their concerns are usually legitimate, they do not understand how they are affecting you. As a congregation, we need to acknowledge that sometimes the people most eager to lead this social justice work are the least adept at doing it, even though they may feel entitled to do so.

Well-intentioned but socially ineffective people have a place at the table—there is room for everyone in this work. However, we need to redirect them from leadership to roles better suited to their talents (perhaps grant writing, research, or logistics). Prophetic leadership roles go to those who can bring people together, spark creativity, and help people manifest their power. We begin by seeking people who are passionate but also poised; we look for optimism, courage, flexibility, patience, persistence, credibility, vision, and humility. Leaders with these qualities can engage others in the work of love by modeling and mentoring qualities such as listening, empowering, vision-casting, communicating clearly, focusing amidst chaos, and demonstrating a love of humanity. That is, we must learn to empower people who have the skills, discipline, and vision to nurture the fullness of our humanity. These are the people who can help us stay in right relationship with one another as we work to improve our world. By so doing, they help our work grow in strength, vision, and relevance.

In our highly intellectual culture, where the power of the mind consistently overshadows the power of the heart, Unitarian Universalists need to remember why love is the only doctrine we would ever claim. Let us venture out of our libraries, classrooms, coffee houses, and churches and spend more time meeting our neighbors, joining community groups, listening to the stories of people with little political power, inviting people to church, sharing our gifts with the community, and engaging the full range of our emotions. We need not minimize our intellectual insight; rather, we must complement that strength with the power of our hearts and ears—especially when it comes to encountering people from groups that have not historically sat in our pews. We need to learn firsthand what love sounds like when it speaks in public.

The love that guided Dr. King all his life is the very type of love that must guide us now. Although he warned us of the possibility of annihilation, he also reminded us that there is a unifying force within each of us. Awakening this force and drawing on it are the keys to our future as a nation and as a denomination. We must develop leaders who can hold us accountable to living it.

When we allow love a central place in the work of justice, we discover a vital new source of inspiration, comfort, sustenance, and deep joy. As we grow in strength, vision, and relevance, we learn that we are all participating in a greater love that ultimately shapes all creation. This experience is what draws people into the pews of First Unitarian Church of Portland, and this is the best practice I can imagine commending to anyone. In the words of John Wesley:

> Love as much as you can,
> By all the means you can,
> In all the ways you can,
> In all the places you can,
> At all the times you can,
> As long as ever you can.

Community, Meaning and Justice

ROB KEITHAN

I am a practical person; I like to get things done. Lately I have enjoyed the challenges of building custom shelving, spice racks in particular. Each design must blend function and form, as the racks must hold jars of various sizes, fit in the space available, and look good doing so. Looking back, my first creation seems simple: just a straightforward rack with a few compartments. My latest spice rack, a housewarming and thank you gift for a friend, hangs in the shape of Philadelphia, a form like a thick Y with one of the arms truncated. The project was harder than I expected, but also more rewarding, and my friend tells me it fits the space perfectly and looks good.

I approach Unitarian Universalist justice work in much the same way I approach woodwork. In both endeavors I seek to balance beauty and effectiveness, creativity and efficiency, form and function. I approach the job in ways that will build capacity and momentum for future projects. In both arenas, my attention never strays far from fit, form, and function. In the case of UU justice work, I constantly ask myself about fit: How does this effort hang together with my religious understanding, our common religious life? I consider form: How should we go about the work, keeping in mind other important UU commitments, such as authentic community and our free and responsible search for truth and meaning? I ask about function: What does it mean to do justice in this case?

I try to answer these questions by drawing on what I have learned from my lifetime in Unitarian Universalism, scores of volunteer commitments, and ten years of advocacy and organizing as legislative director and then director of the UUA Washington Office for Advocacy.

Justice work must fit our religious life. James Luther Adams, Unitarian minister and one of the most influential liberal theologians of the twentieth century, said that liberal religious people come to church seeking two things from the religious life: intimacy and ultimacy. *Intimacy* refers to the human relationships, trust, and support that lead to a sense of belonging. I prefer the term *community*, which maintains Adams's interpersonal focus while encompassing a broader range of group dynamics and activities. Symbolically, we may view intimacy or community as the horizontal dimension of religious life: —.

Ultimacy refers to connection and relationship with something greater than oneself, the depths of our nature and existence. Although it might extend beyond Adams's original intent, I prefer the term *meaning*, which covers both ultimate matters of existence and our human desire for depth in everyday life. Because it connects us to the heights (the sacred, our aspirations, creativity, and insight) and to the depths (our core values, our authentic identities, the significance underlying our days), ultimacy or meaning represents the vertical dimension of religious life: |.

While I agree with Adams that community and meaning, which together may be symbolized by a plus sign (+), are two of the most important reasons people participate in religious community, a third element connects our religious life to the larger world. Without this missing component, our religious life is too isolated and incomplete. What is missing is justice.

Taken together, community, meaning, and justice represent the core of our UU religious life. The symbol I have chosen for justice, a circle (O), represents our inherent connectedness as humans and as beings on this planet. When combined with the two elements Adams named, this circle is drawn around community and meaning, recognizing that their pursuit takes place in the context of the larger world. The three symbols combine to illustrate that community, meaning, and justice are pieces of the same whole: ⊕.

Justice is a broad concept, encompassing values such as equality, fairness, and sustainability. Nearly all of our individual commitments and decisions—what we hold dear, how we act, where we spend our time and money—influence the amount of justice in the world. Our impact is multiplied when we come together as part of a denomination or a single congregation. When we do this—even if we are seeking only meaning and community—we exponentially increase our impact on justice. We buy land and operate buildings. We hire and pay staff. We consume goods and services. In these and countless other decisions in our UU congregational, district, and associational life, our impact on justice is unavoidable.

We can, however, choose the nature of our contribution. Our UU history, though far from perfect, and our UU theology—from our commitment to individual worth to our reverence and responsibility for the natural world—call us to justice work. We must ask what we should do to promote justice in the world.

This brings us from fit to form. Since justice is a part of our religious life, yet cannot substitute for it, the work of justice must also promote meaning and community. This is one of the key differences between activism carried out in our religious setting and activism that happens in a secular context. Linking the three components together situates the function of justice work within the form of Unitarian Universalism.

Ultimately, our progress in each of these areas depends on our willingness to learn and make better choices as a result. Are we willing to consider new information and ideas about how the world works, and our place in it? Will we make changes in what we believe and how we live?

In asking these questions, we can consult the fourth Principle of Unitarian Universalism, wherein our congregations covenant to affirm and promote "a free and responsible search for truth and meaning." The word *responsible* reminds me that I must be continually open to learning and growth. To engage in a responsible search for truth and meaning, I must allow for—and ideally, desire—new information and ideas to transform my ideas, my actions, and my identity.

One particular example comes to mind. I was raised with good, healthy UU values, including affirmation of people's right to their opinions. I also believed that the right of conscience implied the right to share my opinion—to answer as many questions as I could, to offer my ideas, whether or not they were solicited or helpful. In short, I felt entitled to speak. Eventually, thanks to antiracism and antioppression training, I learned that this sense of entitlement is common in affluent, educated white males. As a result, men like me tend to dominate conversations. This habit is annoying at best. At worst, it directly perpetuates oppression, because it can mean there is less room for women, people of color, and other people with historically marginalized identities to speak. In challenging myself to say less, I make room for others to say more. I also learn more, because rather than thinking about what important thing I am going to say next, I can actually listen to what other people are saying.

In U.S. society, and perhaps within Unitarian Universalism especially, our pursuit of transformation tends to overemphasize one of two extremes. Either we concentrate on personal change without much regard for larger social factors, or we focus on changing society without paying sufficient heed to our individual lives and needs. Former UUA president William Sinkford once described the dangers inherent in each imbalance. He said that self-focus can slip into narcissism and that outward focus can slip into arrogance. We pursue personal transformation and social transformation most effectively when we recognize the fundamental link between the personal and the social. What each individual does affects the world, and what happens in the world affects each individual, in an ongoing, dynamic process of change. Thomas Groome, in his book *Christian Religious Education*, warns of the danger to justice-seeking organizations when they fail to make the connection between personal and social:

> If the [group] is to be any more than a reflection of the broader social/cultural environment within which it exists, then a dialectical relationship must be promoted between the two. Otherwise, we become part of the "plausibility structure" that legitimates society as it is, rather than a creative influence for its transformation.

To best influence transformation, we must learn to consider the personal and the social simultaneously, think critically about their dynamic relationship, and locate our own experiences as individuals and groups within the larger cultural context. I have learned to situate my personal experience and socialization as a white male within the larger context of race and racism, sex and sexism. In so doing, I perceive myself and my place in the world differently. I understand that I have other—and better—choices.

We risk being part of the plausibility structure when we seek community and meaning without justice, or justice without community and meaning. All three goals should be pursued throughout our religious life. I offer the following questions as a starting point for evaluating whether a given church program or activity promotes community, meaning, and justice.

To evaluate community we can ask: How does this program or activity build trust and relationships? Do participants introduce themselves and share anything about how they are doing or feeling? Do they interact with each other personally in any meaningful way?

Meaning can be assessed by asking, How does this program or activity encourage spiritual growth? Are participants encouraged to think critically about their experiences, beliefs, and values in ways that connect individual stories with our UU religion and the larger social context?

And to evaluate justice, we can ask, How does this program or activity promote equality, fairness, and sustainability? Who benefits from it? How does it serve people with historically marginalized identities? Does it empower people and encourage systemic change?

The practice that perhaps best embodies all three goals is the term Brazilian educator Paulo Friere (1921–1997) called *praxis*. He argued that we do not learn sufficiently through action alone but through an ongoing cycle of action and reflection. The objective is to reflect critically on information, experiences, and our place in the world, thus linking the personal and the social. The goal of praxis is "critical consciousness": understanding ourselves and our context enough to make deliberate, informed choices.

Although UU curricula and religious education programs have emphasized praxis for years, the practice has not yet been implemented throughout our congregational and associational life. Praxis could be easily carried out almost anywhere, without any supplies, handouts, LCD projectors, or experts. All it takes is asking a group to think critically and talk about their experiences—in church meetings, in the street after the march, in the parking lot after serving meals in the soup kitchen, in the halls of the state capital after a lobbying visit. "Praxis happens" might never be a popular bumper sticker, but I hope to get to the point where it will take place throughout our movement.

Alida DeCoster's essay in this volume describes how in the UUA Washington Office for Advocacy we set aside time each week for praxis, or theological reflection. Sometimes we use a simple reading or personal story to focus on a general topic; other times we focus on our priority policy issue. Each of these issue-oriented theological reflections generally has three parts. First, we review and discuss our UU history and theology on the issue (often we read excerpts from sermons or review relevant statements passed by our General Assemblies). Second, we locate ourselves in the issue by discussing our personal feelings and perspectives. Third, we consider how the issue is playing out in the current culture and policy environment. What messages are out there? Who are the major players? Where do we fit in?

While this could easily lead to a strategic planning session, we save that kind of discussion for another time. The point of reflection is to gain perspective, not lay out a campaign. However, these theological reflections prepare us well for more task-focused work. Taking time to reflect on the connections between an issue and our faith helps ensure that our efforts and messages are firmly and authentically grounded in Unitarian Universalism. In other words, we link community, meaning, and justice, learning about the components required for the fit, in order to choose a form. Strengthening our theological grounding makes our external work more effective because it improves our ability to speak with a religious voice. This is especially important when, as is frequently the case, we are one of very few religious groups on our side of the issue. Often, our secular partners want and need us to bring a clear and powerful faith-based message to the cause. Theological reflection helps make this possible.

There is too much brokenness in our world—too much oppression, too much separation, too much suffering. There is too much work for us to do alone. Fortunately, our faith helps us call to our senses the world's great beauty and vast potential and the fact that we are not alone. In Unitarian Universalism, we have an incredibly powerful resource for personal and social change. By adopting community, meaning, and justice as the goals for our UU life; by developing critical consciousness; by utilizing praxis as a mechanism for discovering the best fit and form for the function of our justice work; and by working in partnership with other groups, we can, slowly, gradually, and incrementally, transform our lives and our world.

Benediction

Who is the prophet in these urgent times?
You are the prophet, for there may be no other who will speak and act now.
The prophet hears and responds to an insistent and urgent inner voice.
The prophet speaks from an internal fountain, giving voice to another's silence.
The prophet sees and expresses in uncommon ways, upsetting the status quo.
The prophet sends the wake-up call in the present, to shape the future.

How do I develop a prophetic voice in these challenging times?
Observe nature and grow all parts of the tree: branches, trunk, and roots.

Branches are the many outspreading ways of acting on inner call.

> Stay connected to the trunk, for fallen limbs are swept away by water or fire.
> Be willing to pare away when too many branches grow.
> Let leaves drop in their time, for the cycle will turn round.
> Grow and let go to flourish, trusting other seasons will come.

The trunk is steady with circles of community, rings of support widening with age.
Witness strong branches supported by many layers.
Observe that when limbs are damaged, the trunk perseveres.
See small trunks grow light shoots, wisely testing support.
Believe that a trunk will mature over time, sending nourishment upward.

Roots are the grounding of the whole tree, the foundation for transformation.
Plant wisely in rich earth for sustenance.
Gather nutrients from a distance in unseen waters.
Sustain the roots through underground connections and keep the trunk standing.
Weather many seasons, drawing on multiple sources for food.

How will we hear the prophets in our complex era?
Follow the still, small voice, even when unpopular.
Offer inner knowing to the outer landscape.
Bear clear witness to the claims of many sacred traditions.
Cultivate strength and compassion.
Develop wisdom that is tenacious, and flexible when needed.
Watch, wait, and choose the strategic moment.
Disrupt or challenge when there is clarity of vision.
Send a startling message through crafted purpose.
Say what is not welcome, at the right time.
Speak boldly about what the majority wants to ignore.
Practice faithfulness, foresee consequences, make history.
Offer gratitude, for in oneness with other trees, a forest grows.

—Louise Green

For Further Reading

George K. Beach, *Transforming Liberalism: The Theology of James Luther Adams*, Skinner House, 2005.

Marjorie Bowens-Wheatley and Nancy Palmer Jones, eds., *Soul Work: Anti-Racist Theologies in Dialogue*, Skinner House, 2002.

Rita Nakashima Brock and Rebecca Ann Parker, *Saving Paradise: How Christianity Traded Love of This World for Crucifixion and Empire*, Beacon, 2008.

Amy Chau, *World on Fire: How Exporting Free Market Democracy Breeds Ethnic Hatred and Global Instability*, Doubleday, 2003.

Carl Dudley, *Community Ministry: New Challenges, Proven Steps to Faith-Based Initiatives*, Alban, 2002.

Dorothy May Emerson, ed., *Standing Before Us: Unitarian Universalist Women and Social Reform, 1776–1936*, Skinner House, 1999.

Jill Andresky Fraser, *White Collar Sweatshop: The Deterioration of Work and Its Rewards in Corporate America*, W. W. Norton & Company, 2001.

Richard S. Gilbert, *How Much Do We Deserve? An Inquiry into Distributive Justice*, Skinner House, 2000.

———, *The Prophetic Imperative: Social Gospel in Theory and Practice*, Skinner House, 2000.

Ronald A. Heifetz et al., *The Practice of Adaptive Leadership: Tools and Tactics for Changing Your Organization and the World*, Harvard Business Press, 2009.

Jacqui James and Judith Frediani, *Weaving the Fabric of Diversity: An Anti-bias Program for Adults*, UUA, 1996.

Allan G. Johnson, *Privilege, Power, and Difference* (2nd edition), McGraw-Hill, 2005.

Tony Johnson, ed., *Urban Discipleship: The Theology and Praxis in the Veatch Urban Social Justice Ministry Project*, Faithful Fools Copy Shop, 2006.

Jacqueline J. Lewis, *The Power of Stories: A Guide for Leading Multiracial and Multicultural Congregations*, Abingdon, 2008.

Paul Rogat Loeb, *The Impossible Will Take a Little While: A Citizen's Guide to Hope in a Time of Fear*, Basic Books, 2004.

John Gibb Millspaugh, "Justice: Understanding Social Action," "Justice: How UUs Make a Difference," and "Social Action Projects," *Coming of Age Manual: Handbook for Congregations*, Sarah Gibb Millspaugh, UUA, 2009, pp. 163–174, 207–216.

Stephanie Y. Mitchem, *Introducing Womanist Theology*, Orbis, 2002.

Leslie Takahashi Morris, Chip Roush, and Leon Spencer, *The Arc of the Universe Is Long: Unitarian Universalists, Anti-Racism and the Journey from Calgary*, Skinner House, 2009.

Mark D. Morrison-Reed and Jacqui James, eds., *Been in the Storm So Long: A Meditation Manual*, 1991.

Rebecca Ann Parker, *Blessing the World: What Can Save Us Now*, edited by Robert Hardies, Skinner House, 2006.

Anthony Pinn, *Terror and Triumph: The Nature of Black Religion*, Augsburg Fortress, 2003.

Paul Rasor, *Faith without Certainty: Liberal Theology in the 21st Century*, Skinner House, 2005.

Jill Schwendeman, *When Youth Lead: A Guide to Intergenerational Social Justice Ministry*, Skinner House, 2007.

Marilyn Sewell, *Unitarian Universalist Culture: The Present and the Promise*, Fuller Press, 2006.

Stephen M. Shick, *Be the Change: Poems, Prayers and Meditations for Peacemakers and Justice Seekers*, 2009.

Thandeka, "Future Designs for Liberal Theology," *Journal of American Theology and Philosophy* (January 2009) 20:1.

———, "New Words for Life," *A Language of Reverence*, edited by Dean Grodzins, Meadville Lombard, 2004.

UUA, *Congregation-Based Community Organizing: A Social Justice Approach to Revitalizing Congregational Life*, 2006, available from www.uua.org/documents/aw/cbco_booklet.pdf

UUA, *Social Justice Empowerment Program Handbook*, 2008, available from www.uua.org/documents/aw/sje_handbook.pdf

UUA, *Unitarian Universalism and the Quest for Racial Justice, 1967–1982*, UUA, 1993.

UUA, *The Welcoming Congregation Handbook: Resources for Affirming Bisexual, Gay, Lesbian and/or Transgender People*, Skinner House, 1999.

Sharon D. Welch, *Real Peace, Real Security: The Challenges of Global Citizenship*, Fortress, 2008.

About the Contributors

Taquiena Boston is the director of identity-based ministries at the Unitarian Universalist Association (UUA). Prior to assuming this role, she was an antiracism program associate in the Faith in Action staff group of the UUA. Taquiena's professional experience also includes fund-raising, communications, and organizational change work for nonprofit organizations in the arts, education, youth services, health care, energy efficiency, and religion. She writes about the Black Arts Movement in Washington DC, teaches Latin dance, and performs with the Ashe Moyubba Afro-Cuban dance company and the Joy of Motion Broadway jazz summer workshop. She is a longtime member of All Souls Church, Unitarian, in Washington DC.

Carol Caouette is the assistant to the music director at White Bear Unitarian Universalist Church in Mahtomedi, Minnesota. She has been the principal collaborative pianist there since 1998. She has studied classical piano and voice, English literature, and education and is a licensed language arts teacher for grades 7 to 12. She is working toward a master of fine arts degree in creative writing.

Alida DeCoster, a former parish minister who served in Bethesda, Maryland, has been the minister to the Social Justice Internship Program at the UUA Washington Office for Advocacy since 2003, leading weekly theological reflection. She is also a spiritual director, having completed the Shalem Institute Spiritual Guidance Program in 2005. She meets with Unitarian Universalists (UUs) one on one for discernment, reflection, and prayer.

Adam G. Gerhardstein is the campaign manager of the UUA's Standing on the Side of Love Campaign, which advocates against exclusion, oppression, and violence based on identity. In 2008–2009 he served as the acting director of the UUA Washington Office for Advocacy. In 2005, he graduated from Xavier University with a bachelor's degree focusing on international issues. In 2001 he founded Ugali, an organization that supports communities and students in Western Kenya. He grew up in the First Unitarian Church of Cincinnati, and is currently a member of All Souls Church, Unitarian, in Washington DC, where he is active in its social justice ministries.

Louise Green has been the minister of social justice at All Souls Church, Unitarian, in Washington DC since 2004. Louise completed her master of divinity degree at Harvard Divinity School in 1991 and was ordained in 1992 in the United Church of Christ. She has served as associate minister in United Church of Christ congregations in Sudbury, Massachusetts, and in New York City. Louise was a lead community organizer with the Industrial Areas Foundation for eight years in Manhattan and Brooklyn, New York. Currently she is working on a master's degree in applied healing arts at Tai Sophia Institute in Maryland.

Robert M. Hardies is senior minister of All Souls Church, Unitarian, in Washington DC and a leader in the Washington Interfaith Network, a coalition of churches building power to create social change. He also serves on the Board and Executive Committee of La Clinica del Pueblo, a health clinic serving the District's Latino immigrant community, and on the Advisory Board of the Network of Spiritual Progressives. His commentaries have appeared in *Utne Reader*, *Shambala Sun*, Tikkun.org, and frequently on the public radio program *Interfaith Voices*. Recently, All Souls was featured as an exemplary progressive congregation on CNN's *Anderson Cooper 360* and the PBS series *I Believe*.

MARK A. HICKS is the Angus MacLean professor of religious education at Meadville Lombard Theological School in Chicago. Prior to this appointment he was an associate professor of educational transformation at George Mason University in Arlington, Virginia. He holds a doctorate in philosophy and education and a master's degree in adult development in higher education, both from Columbia University in New York City. Mark consults nationally with schools and government and nonprofit organizations on building inclusive, democratically minded, multiracial, and multicultural learning communities. He is a lay leader at All Souls Church, Unitarian, in Washington DC and the Riverside Church in New York City.

PAULA COLE JONES, a past president of Diverse and Revolutionary Unitarian Universalist Multicultural Ministries, is lead consultant for JUUST Change, an antioppression consultancy program for UU congregations, and a facilitator for Beyond Categorical Thinking workshops. She served two years as cochair of the Senior Minister Search Committee at All Souls Church, Unitarian, in Washington DC, which resulted in the successful call of Robert Hardies. She is founder of A Dialogue on Race and Ethnicity (ADORE), cochair of the Baltimore-Washington Region Growth Committee's Diversity Team, and co-chair of the Joseph Priestley District's Journey Toward Wholeness Transformation Team.

ROB KEITHAN is director of the UUA Washington Office for Advocacy. In that role he seeks to change national policy and culture on issues of concern to the Association, and to support effective, congregation-based action for justice. He joined the staff of the Washington Office in 1999. He is pursuing a master of divinity degree at Wesley Theological Seminary and is a candidate for Unitarian Universalist ministry. He is a member of All Souls Church, Unitarian, in Washington DC.

NANCY MCDONALD LADD is a graduate of Meadville Lombard Theological School and has served as minister to the Bull Run Unitarian Universalists of Manassas, Virginia, since 2004. She currently serves as president of the Chesapeake Area UU Ministers Association, and her writing appears in the recent Jenkin Lloyd Jones Press publication, *Reverend X: How Generation X Ministers Are Shaping Unitarian Universalism.*

KAT LIU is assistant director of the UUA Washington Office for Advocacy, where she is primarily responsible for providing electronic communications and resources to UU congregations and individuals engaged in legislative advocacy. She also holds the Environmental Justice portfolio—trying to bring a social justice lens to environmental issues. In a previous life, Kat was a biologist; she left that profession to pursue a degree in religious studies.

KATE LORE has been directing the social justice program at First Unitarian Church of Portland, Oregon, for the past ten years. She received her master of divinity degree from Meadville/Lombard School of Theology in 2007. Kate brings sixteen years of church leadership into her ministry and specializes in community organizing, leadership development, conflict resolution, and creative networking.

DAN MCKANAN is the Ralph Waldo Emerson UUA senior lecturer at Harvard Divinity School. He has written three books on religious movements for social transformation in the United States and is currently at work on a general history of the religious left, to be published by Beacon Press. Dan's activism has included extending hospitality to people experiencing homelessness, holding male batterers accountable for their violence, and working to transform global economic institutions such as the World Bank and International Monetary Fund.

John Gibb Millspaugh is a graduate of the John F. Kennedy School of Government and Harvard Divinity School. He served as assistant for public witness to UUA president John Buehrens for three years. As minister of the UU congregation in Mission Viejo, California, he became the *Orange County Register*'s go-to liberal religious voice on controversial issues, and his speech on marriage equality was broadcast nationwide on C-SPAN. John currently serves as chair of the Core Team for the new Congregational Study/Action Issue, Ethical Eating: Food and Environmental Justice. In the fall of 2008, he accepted the call of Winchester Unitarian Society in Winchester, Massachusetts, to serve as co-minister with his spouse, Sarah Gibb Millspaugh.

Peter Morales is the president of the UUA. Before beginning his term in 2009, he served as senior minister at Jefferson Unitarian Church in Golden, Colorado. He also served for two years as the UUA's director of district services. Morales is a former member of the UUA Board of Trustees and of the Unitarian Universalist Ministers Association Executive Team—as the first person to carry the new antiracism, antioppression, multiculturalism portfolio. Before entering the ministry, he worked as a newspaper journalist in Oregon. He was a Knight International Press Fellow in Peru and is a former Fulbright lecturer in American Studies in Spain. He and Phyllis Windrem Morales have been married forty-one years. They have two children, Miguel and Marcela.

Rebecca Ann Parker is president and professor of theology at Starr King School for the Ministry. She is author of *Blessing the World: What Can Save Us Now*, edited by Robert Hardies, and co-author with Rita Nakashima Brock of *Proverbs of Ashes: Violence, Redemptive Suffering, and the Search for What Saves Us* and *Saving Paradise: How Christianity Traded Love of This World for Crucifixion and Empire.* She is currently working on a primer in liberal theology with John Buehrens, *A House for Hope: Renewing the Promise of Progressive Religion*. Rebecca teaches UU theologies and a core required course, Educating to Counter Oppressions and Create Just and Sustainable Communities. Before coming to Starr King, she spent ten years as a parish minister. She is dually affiliated with the United Methodist Church and the UUA.

Paul Rasor is director of the Center for the Study of Religious Freedom and professor of interdisciplinary studies at Virginia Wesleyan College. He received his doctorate in the study of religion from Harvard and his law degree from the University of Michigan. He also holds a master of divinity degree from Harvard Divinity School and a bachelor of music degree from the University of Michigan School of Music. He is an ordained UU minister. Paul's academic career includes fourteen years as a law professor, as well as ten years teaching in theology and religious studies. His latest book is *Faith without Certainty: Liberal Theology in the 21st Century*. Paul is a classical and jazz trombonist, and he has played with several symphony orchestras and small jazz combos.

Meg Riley received her call to the ministry while caring for abused children in a residential facility. She attended United Theological Seminary of the Twin Cities, graduating with a master's degree in religious studies in 1987. During and after seminary, she worked in three congregations in the Twin Cities as a director of religious education. In 1989, Meg joined the staff at the UUA headquarters as youth programs director. She has worked at the UUA ever since, serving as director of lesbian, bisexual, and gay concerns and director of the Washington Office for Advocacy before assuming her current position as director of advocacy and witness programs. Meg is also president of Faith in Public Life: A Resource Center for Justice and the Common Good. She has served on the boards of the Interfaith Alliance, Equal Partners in Faith, Americans United for Separation of Church and State, and Interfaith Workers for Justice and on the steering committees of dozens of national coalitions.

VICTORIA SAFFORD has been minister of White Bear Unitarian Universalist Church in Mahtomedi, Minnesota, since 1999, following a ten-year ministry in Northampton, Massachusetts, prior to which she was a community organizer with the American Friends Service Committee. A graduate of Vassar College and Yale Divinity School, she is the author of numerous articles and essays and a meditation manual called *Walking toward Morning*. Her essay "The Small Work in the Great Work" appears in Paul Rogat Loeb's anthology, *The Impossible Will Take a Little While.*

JILL SCHWENDEMAN is director of youth programs at White Bear Unitarian Universalist Church in Mahtomedi, Minnesota. She served as executive director for two nonprofit coalitions in Illinois, North Suburban Peace Initiative and Families' and Children's AIDS Network. She has designed award-winning social action initiatives around issues including homelessness, prostitution, and HIV/AIDS. Schwendeman is co-author of *There Is Hope: Learning to Live with HIV* and author of *When Youth Lead: Intergenerational Social Justice Ministry*. She holds a master of divinity degree from the University of Chicago.

MARILYN SEWELL is the minister emerita of the First Unitarian Church of Portland, Oregon, where she served for 17 years until her recent retirement. She holds master's degrees in English literature, social work, and divinity, and a Ph.D. in theology and literature from the Graduate Theological Union and the University of California at Berkeley. She is also the recipient of an honorary doctorate from Meadville Lombard Theological School. She is the editor of two books of women's poetry, *Cries of the Spirit* and its companion volume, *Claiming the Spirit Within*. She edited two volumes of essays, *Resurrecting Grace: Remembering Catholic Childhoods* and *Breaking Free: Women of Spirit at Midlife and Beyond.* Her two most recent publications are *A Little Book on Forgiveness* and *A Little Book on Prayer*.

William Sinkford served as the seventh president of the UUA from 2001 until 2009. His presidency was distinguished by efforts to defend oppressed peoples. He was an outspoken critic of the war in Iraq, a nationally recognized champion of equal marriage rights for same-sex couples, and a passionate advocate for the people of Darfur. Under Sinkford's leadership, the UUA became the first national denomination to join the New Sanctuary Movement, and formally voted to work to combat global warming. He was a staunch defender of religious pluralism and the separation of church and state. Sinkford freely shared his own spiritual journey and called on Unitarian Universalism to reclaim a language of reverence. He currently serves as senior minister and advisor at the Unitarian Universalist Urban Ministry in Boston.

Thandeka is an ordained Unitarian Universalist minister and theologian. She is the founder of Affect Theology, which investigates the links between religion and emotions using insights from affective neuroscience. She is the author of *The Embodied Self: Friedrich Schleiermacher's Solution to Kant's Problem of the Empirical Self* and *Learning to be White: Money, Race and God in America* and is a contributor to books including *The Cambridge Companion to Schleiermacher* and *The Oxford Handbook on Feminist Theology and Globalization* (forthcoming). Thandeka's current book project is *Affect Theology: Returning Rational Theology to its Senses.* Her numerous publications in journals include essays in *American Journal of Theology and Philosophy*, *The International Journal of Practical Theology*, *Harvard Theological Review*, *Process Studies*, and *Tikkun.*

Sharon D. Welch is provost and professor of religion and society at Meadville Lombard Theological School in Chicago. She received her doctorate from Vanderbilt University in 1982 and has held positions as associate professor of theology, religion, and society at Harvard Divinity School and as professor and chair of religious studies, professor of women's and gender studies, and adjunct professor of educational leadership and policy analysis at the University of Missouri. While at the University of Missouri, Sharon was a senior fellow in the Center for Religion, the Professions, and the Public; a project leader of the Ford-sponsored Difficult Dialogues Program; and cochair of the Committee for the Scholarship of Multicultural Teaching and Learning. Sharon is currently a member of the International Steering Committee of Global Action to Prevent War. She is also the author of several books, including *A Feminist Ethic of Risk*, *After Empire: The Art and Ethos of Enduring Peace*, and her latest, *The Challenges of Global Citizenship*. She was awarded the honorary degree of doctor of sacred theology by Starr King School of the Ministry in May 2007.

Acknowledgments

A People So Bold, in its book and DVD versions, would not have been possible without the vision and support of the All Souls-Beckner Advancement Fund—established through a donation from Earl and Meta Beckner in 1973 to All Souls Church, Unitarian, in Washington DC—and the Unitarian Universalist Funding Program's Fund for Unitarian Universalism. These grants subsidized the Social Justice and Theology Convocation in Baltimore, where the essays in this book were first delivered as papers. The convocation was jointly hosted by All Souls Church, Unitarian, and the UUA.

Also, thanks go to the churches, universities, and seminaries that lent their leaders' time to this project, and to all the participants at the convocation for sharing so generously of their intellectual and spiritual capital. This includes not only the contributors to this volume, but also Mary Benard, Dr. Charlie Clements, Gini Courter, Hillary Goodridge, Rev. Dr. Laurel Hallman, Susan Leslie, Rev. Harlan Limpert, Annalease Hastings, Steve and Chris Sealy, and Rev. Ned Wight.

Most of all, we dwell in gratitude for the religious impulse that moves so many Unitarian Universalists to find and express their faith through their work for justice.